WAKE UP to Your Stories:

Using the Art of Personal Narrative to Heal Your Past, Nurture Your Relationships & Ask for What You're Worth

ALYSON MEAD

A Storied Life
New York Los Angeles

PUBLISHED BY A STORIED LIFE

Book design by Suzanne Raney — Raney Day Designs

Library of Congress Cataloging-In-Publication Data

Mead, Alyson, 1962-

Wake Up to Your Stories/Alyson Mead.—1st US ed.

cm.

1. Storytelling—Culture—United States
2. Meditation—Spirituality   3. Writing—How To

PRINTED IN THE UNITED STATES OF AMERICA

First U.S. Edition: September 2006

ISBN 1-4276-0094-5

1   3   5   7   9   10   8   6   4   2

For Noel, who makes the mundane an adventure

Contents

Introduction

"The universe is made of stories, not of atoms."

— Muriel Rukeyser

While I was growing up, my family didn't have a lot of money. Both of my parents were elementary school teachers, and divorced when I was four. My brother and I went to live with our mother, a natural born storyteller. She could keep her classroom of rowdy children rapt as she turned a history lesson into a game, or a lecture about current events into a chance for students to relate these often-dry and historical news blurbs to things that had actually happened in their lives. Her kids never noticed that they were learning, and neither did my brother and I.

We lived on the eastern end of Long Island, known for its glamorous homes and famous "Summer People" more than anything else. Our entertainment was often found at the beach. During June, July and August, Dune Road, a thin strip of asphalt paralleling the shore, was too jammed with cars to be much fun. Stressed-out people blared their horns or yelled at one another in an effort to get to the "fun" part of the day a little faster. Riding your bike could be just as dangerous, as the interminable waiting caused some to zoom onto the sandy shoulder or over the hilly dunes, only to find their wheels spinning uselessly.

My favorite times came when the weather was cold and rainy, and the population of my town had shrunk by about fifty percent. The Summer People had packed up their time-shares and gone back into the city, and few, if any, cars passed us on our way to the public beach. When my mom found what she was looking for, she turned the car in and drove up the ascending rectangle of the parking lot, bypassing all of the angled spaces to park at the very top. Turning off the ignition at the edge of the sand, she nodded at a man in the distance.

"What do you think he's doing?" she asked.

I knew what was coming. Her question meant that I was to make up a story about him, which she would embellish. Back and forth we'd bat the story until it had served its purpose of enlightenment, sadness, surprise, or laughter.

"He's a tennis pro," I answered. "See the way he carries that stick over his shoulder, like it's a tennis racket?"

"Yes. But why is he walking alone?"

"He wanted to come down here with his dog, but he had a fight with his wife and she wouldn't let him bring the dog down here."

"She's busy teaching the dog French, so she can have someone to talk to."

"NO! The dog is a Weimeraner. He wants to learn German." I giggled into my hand, watching the man trace a lonely path along the blue-gray shore. "His wife wants to learn French, so she'll seem more cultured at cocktail parties."

"When he gets back home, she'll demand that he take her to France or she'll file for divorce."

"Either that, or she will insist that he stop being a tennis pro so he can go into horticulture." At thirteen, I had no idea what the word meant. I just thought it sounded cool.

"He's a horticulturist working on a rare strain of orchid."

"Yes, but she wants him to be more practical, and invent a new kind of tomato. The kind they'd sell at the Barefoot Contessa."

On and on we went, until the man on the beach finally walked past our car, got into his own vehicle and drove off, casting off the tennis racket stick just before he closed the door.

The afternoon was gone, but my mother and I had formed a bond. We had lived in the space of our minds together, just for awhile, and it had made us friends. By the time I was fourteen, I understood what my own stories meant, and vowed to keep them close to me always.

For my fourteenth birthday, my father gave me a camera. For a time, images became more important than words, and I went on to study art in college, much to the chagrin of the more practical members of my family.

After leaving school, my job choices were limited. I labored in retail stores, in offices and on movie sets. I lived in Boston, New York and Los Angeles, looking for a window into the life I could see in my mind's eye, but could not seem to create in my physical reality. My interest in photography and filmmaking took me to badly paid positions as a Production Assistant on one terrible movie after another. Finally, when I had had enough of trying to scrape together my rent on the first of each month, my roommate found me a job in a publishing company.

It was as if someone had shined headlights on a blacktop at midnight. In helping to create children's books and the educational materials that accompanied them, I could see where I was going. Excitement took the place of fear when I realized that I was part of something wonderful. As a team, my co-workers and I were making a united effort to build a tolerant, multicultural universe in the pages of our books. Money was still hard, but I quickly worked myself into positions that required more advanced editorial skills. I enjoyed going to work for the sole reason that I was able to assist in the birth of new stories every day.

When I moved to Los Angeles, stories continued to permeate my life. I worked on documentaries, feature films and televisions shows. Firsthand, I saw how they came to be created, from the first excitement of ideas through disappointments, tenacity, triumph, and occasionally failure. Though largely unintentional, in trying to reach the widest audience, producers and executives often "dumbed down" scripts, diluting or abandoning the original charm or magic of the piece. These people who had been driven to tell stories in the first place had managed to pull the rug out from under themselves, and from under us, as audience members. That was not for me.

Since then, I have made a career as a freelance writer, looking for meaningful, though sometimes underreported, stories to tell, in articles, essays, books and screenplays. I have been widely published, won awards, and found larger audiences. Even on bad days, when it seems like there's nothing left to say, I wake up infused with energy. There is galvanizing anger, to correct injustices, or share the slow spread of sadness in a poignant tale. Some stories make me laugh, or remind me of my own fragile humanity. I let the world tell me its stories, and agree to act as its vessel.

Most of us live variations on this theme, though we may live in far-flung parts of the world, or have jobs that require varying skills. Stories are everywhere, and if we take the time to look for them, we will realize that they permeate all of us, no matter which social, economic or ethnic groups we may belong to. From the time we first come home from the hospital or birthing center, stories surround us. Our caretakers may lean over the edge of our cribs as they tuck us in for the night, telling us tales, or singing stories to us in lullabies. It is through our stories that we learn where we have come from, and where we might be headed if we follow the paths of our destinies. Through the medium of story, we are instantly connected with ancestors and their customs, in ways that may never otherwise touch our lives.

As we grow, we carry these stories with us, through our schooling, into our teenage and adult years. We have them while we do errands, ride the subway, or take part in leisure activities. We may even tell these stories to our own children, our mates and our friends, who each occupy an important role in our community.

For a time, we are free to make up stories that our parents will tolerate or even encourage, only too happy to help us develop our imaginations. But somewhere between the end of our schooling and the time when issues of work and family take over our lives, we forget the stories that have kept us company on our journey. We are asked to become responsible, and stories, the purview of children, are whisked away from us. Worries are superimposed over them, about building a solid career, or being able to pay our mortgage at the beginning of each month. We may have to strive to afford health insurance, find better schools for our children, or to gain the respect of our colleagues. Some of us may shift our focus to dating, and endeavor to form committed relationships. We may wish to get married and have children, or cultivate relationships with teachers and friends. Spirituality may also take a chunk of our time, as we struggle to make sense of ourselves and the world around us.

As we forget our stories, we begin to lose our sense of connection with others, from the ancestors who came before us to our family members who may still be living. We may forget what it feels like to connect to friends and co-workers, high school sweethearts, or the butcher who used to save the best cuts of meat for our mothers. Our memories are dulled, like a tool that goes rusty from lack of use.

In this way, we begin to break away from our communities. Our stories are replaced with rushed cell phone calls, or emails dashed off before a meeting. We watch television or DVDs instead of discussing the issues of our days, whether mundane or earth-shattering. Inexorably, we fall asleep as we move further and further from the very process that accompanied us into the world, and which continues to ground us when everything else may appear to be collapsing.

In this sleep state, most of us live our lives. Though we may profess a desire to live more passionately, or experience things on a more profound level, by cutting off the source of our passion, our well of deep experience, we make it impossible to do this. Our spiritual work, our community service and love for our families, while still valuable, are dampened by the way we perform our tasks. We rush our way through them to get to the finish line, wherever that is.

The sleep state we live in helps us to keep the film, television and publishing businesses going, to the tune of several hundred billion dollars per year. They cater to the world of illusion, and we are happy to comply. We spend billions more each year to stay fit, look younger and trim our waistlines, allowing other people to tell us how to live, what to think, and even how to relate to our own bodies. By forgetting our stories, we have relinquished the mantle of critical thinking, and have instead become content to make uninformed decisions, using little real information and emotional intelligence.

Only in waking up to our stories can we begin to regain

that sense of connection that allows our sense of wonder and magic to exist alongside our responsibilities. Remembering our stories, and making a conscious effort to share them with others, can make our lives more fulfilling, nurture relationships with family members and friends, and even build self-esteem for accomplishing life tasks and greater goals.

Wake Up to Your Stories is designed to help you connect with your personal stories over the course of eleven weeks. You are welcome to move through the stages faster or slower, depending on the amount of time you may have to devote to each one of them. The program does not require you to be a writer, or even have a desire to publish your writing, though many of you will be in a very good position to do that by the end of these eleven weeks, should you wish to do so.

Wake Up to Your Stories is not a writing book, but it will employ methods used by writers. It will not go over sentence structure, grammar or potential markets in which to sell your work. But it will encourage you to record your experience on this planet, and to explore how this connects to your own needs and desires as a human being.

If you are already writing, or want to begin a writing practice, this book will be able to help you unlock the stories inside you, which can become the foundation for future fiction or non-fiction works. Whether your stories are headed for the silver screen, the pages of a book, or a series of epistles to a dead relative, Wake Up to Your Stories can help you sharpen the tools used by successful writers everywhere.

Wake Up to Your Stories is not a book about spirituality, but it will help you connect with your own sense of the spiritual, and use this to deepen the meaning of your stories, for yourself and others. It will borrow from many disciplines, but require no religious beliefs, or adherence to any particular tradition. Along the way, though, you may find yourself believing in yourself more than you ever have before.

Wake Up to Your Stories is about living your most authentic life, every day. The path of storytelling requires bravery, and the desire to look more deeply into ourselves than we are normally encouraged to do. It is about coming into contact, maybe for the first time, with the storylines that have formulated our experience. In doing this, we can begin to rewrite the parts we may want to change.

The program outlined in Wake Up to Your Stories is about the courage it takes to own up to past mistakes, and be ready to render apologies, even if they're only on paper for now. A yoga teacher I know gives a great instruction during class. He says, "Think about yourself being breathed, instead of trying to breathe a certain way." This book is similar in nature. It's about allowing ourselves to be breathed by our stories, to be filled up with our own essence and history in order to make the changes we want to make. Far from becoming passive, we will strike a balance between vigilance and laziness, hard and soft, disciplined and casual. We will exist intentionally, allowing ourselves to be lived.

I am not promising success without work. The meditations and exercises in this book require you to carve out time for yourself, which may be the hardest step of all for many of us. But storytelling is a gift and, as with any gift, we should learn to accept it gracefully. Making time for ourselves is never wrong. In fact, it may be the only thing that can truly reconnect us with our lost selves, and make everything we do come from the purest place of love and acceptance.

Telling stories requires being truly awake, and being awake requires effort. It does not mean showing up with your eyes half open, a latte in hand for the buzz it'll provide. Your success will depend on your desire to make this process second nature, until it is fully integrated into the fabric of your life. With that being said, this process is about having fun, and realizing the most uniquely human parts inside all of us.

My life has been filled with stories, and for that I will always be grateful. If you're reading this book, perhaps you have been guided to connect with the stories of your life, too. I want to thank you for taking the time to read it, and to hopefully make your life richer as a result.

Wake Up to Your Stories

Our Silence

"*Long before I wrote stories, I listened for stories. Listening for them is something more acute than listening to them. I suppose it's an early form of participation in what goes on. Listening children know stories are there. When their elders sit and begin, children are just waiting and hoping for one to come out, like a mouse from its hole.*"

— Eudora Welty

These days, we spend less time than ever on the things we want to do. Most of our time is spent working and paying bills, or reaching for the kind of life we see on television, or can imagine in our minds. The remainder of our time is spent on things like spiritual fulfillment, family duties, and cultivating relationships. And barely any of our time is spent on creativity, community activities, or personal growth.

Doing things this way only increases our stress. What we strive for every day may seem to move further and further from our grasp as we kill ourselves trying to reach it. Over time, we become more irritable, with shorter fuses, and find it impossible to even remember what it felt like to be relaxed, or happy, or sane.

Though stress has become a popular buzzword in recent years, almost to the point of overuse, numerous scientific studies have connected it to a profound sense of disconnection. Often, doctors and psychiatrists have discovered that patients reporting high levels of stress have corresponding symptoms such as loneliness, isolation, depression and anxiety. Taken together, these form a picture of modern-day malaise, with each of us feeling we have to fight our battles alone, without showing weakness or burdening anyone else with our troubles.

Trying to hang on to our lives by our fingernails in this way has also been linked to heart attacks and stroke, diabetes, digestive disorders, immune disorders, cancers, eating problems, sexual dysfunction and sleep disturbances, among others.

Where are we trying to go? What are we trying to achieve? And why, despite all of our efforts, does it seem to elude us?

It helps to take a look at how our bodies are affected. When we experience stress, either internally or externally, our bodies immediately produce the "fight or flight response," activating the hypothalamic-pituitary-adrenal (HPA) system and releasing various steroid hormones into our bloodstream. These include cortisol, which has been connected with the epidemic levels of obesity afflicting the U.S. and other countries, and other hormones. In addition, the body releases catecholamines, which are neurotransmitters that carry messages from one part of the brain to another.

These catecholamines activate a part of the brain called the amygadala, which allows us to form an emotional reaction to whatever has caused our stress. The hippocampus then stores this emotional response as a memory, so we don't forget how dangerous tigers are, for example. As our reaction to stress unfolds, our breathing becomes more rapid, our lungs take in more oxygen, and our blood flow increases dramatically, sometimes as much as 300-400%.

Over time, if we continue to experience these stress reactions, our spleens, while discharging red and white blood cells to transport more oxygen to wherever it's needed, begin to suppress the immune system. This occurs in tandem with the hormones being released. Though we may not be facing a tiger, we feel that way, and so our bodies dampen our digestion so we can fight the dangers we perceive are facing us.

Some of our most common stressors include:

- high-pressure work situations
- problems or disappointments in relationships
- loneliness, or feelings of separation
- worries about money and security

For most of us, it's hard not to find at least one thing on this list that sounds very familiar. Not being in control of our marriages, our finances, our social lives or our jobs can produce a range of feelings, from irritation to fear to red-faced anger. But a little bit of these stress reactions can be great for us. They can provide the irritation required to make changes we may be afraid to make any other way. They can give us that little shove we may need to fall in love, leave a dead-end job, or explain to a family member that hearing our old nickname still hurts.

Most doctors agree that the causes of stress derive from one main area. When we feel out of control, or are faced with an unpredictable situation, we will almost always feel unbalanced, as if nothing can be counted on or deciphered. Not being able to use our senses to interpret our world can give rise to hopelessness or anger as we find only confusion and muddled signals. We stumble around, trying to connect to anything meaningful, but our existence often becomes more than we can bear.

The first time many of us can remember feeling that stress, and knowing how to name it, came when we have left school and were asked to be truly responsible for the first time. Usually, this happens during our teenage years, when we leave home, whether to attend school or live on our own, with mates or friends. Though we may be excited about finally getting out from under the repressive gaze of our parents or caregivers, usually we find that meeting the responsibilities of life head-on is not easy.

When we realize that our minimum wage job is going to mean less fun with our friends on weekends or paying the rent late, we have a conundrum on our hands. What kind of people will we become? The kind of person that pays the rent on time, or one that values fun above all else? Why do any of us have to make that hard a decision?

Judgement, therefore, becomes part of the equation almost as soon as we are on our own, and sometimes beforehand. We are all asked to decide the answer to this question, perhaps before we are ready to answer it. I'm not saying that parents are mean and hard-hearted, or never help their kids. I'm also not saying that teenagers have it hard and shouldn't have to work for a living. But this is the point at which our stories start to die. At this time, we may experience physical reactions to stress, such as the ones listed above, or suffer emotional reactions that last into our twenties, thirties or even later. Sometimes, these reactions may stay buried, and become the foundation for other, more pernicious, issues. At this very sensitive time in our lives, when our stories could help us most, and allow us a sense of grounding and support, they dry up or are displaced by practical worries.

Most of us never have the chance to wake up to our stories. We may stumble upon one or two of them in therapy, if we choose this path, or in art, if we have the courage to go in that direction. But we may have no idea how to use them to our greatest benefit.

Our stories may seem unimportant to us. "Who cares what happened to me when I was two?" we might say. Or, "No one's really going to lose sleep if they don't hear about my adventure at the grocery store today."

This is the Parental Voice we all carry inside us. This doesn't necessarily mean that parents are bad, or want to somehow squash our stories out of us. They gave them to us in the first place, so this can't be true. But their job, as many see it, is to watch out for us, and make sure we have the tools to live on our own. It may mean that parents become overly protective of our safety—if you don't believe this now, wait until you have kids, or are around kids for any length of time, and see if it doesn't happen to you. The Parental Voice is actually a distorted and amplified version of what our parents really said, because it contains our interpretation and emotional echoes of what might happen if we go against their wishes.

Our reaction, when faced with this fear, is often silence. Whether we choose to rant and rave in private, or blow off our frustration in other ways, by not facing a person or situation directly, we are inadvertently buying into silence. In the case of relationships, we may not ask for what we want because the other person won't be happy, and might leave us. In our families, we may worry about being ostracized or yelled at if we have something unpleasant or controversial to say. And in the case of our jobs, we are afraid to irritate our bosses, for fear that he or she will not promote us. In the worst case scenario, we may be terrified that our boss will actually fire us for speaking up, even if it's done in an appropriate, professional manner.

In these cases, the Parental Voice has drowned out our Authentic Voice, the one that is open to sharing and discussing, no matter how difficult or controversial a subject may be. This voice is sensitive to other people's feelings, and willing to negotiate with others to find a common solution. It is the way we find common ground as humans, and it is inside every one of us.

Some of us respond to this silence by drinking or taking drugs to dull the pain. Others give away their power to food, gambling, exercise or the people they date. We search for one more great meal or lover so we don't have to think about the things we wanted to do and didn't. We avoid looking into mirrors for fear of what we will find there. But the problem lies in our not being able to make a true connection with our desires, and not being able to see a clear path to achieving what we want.

For instance, we may know that we want more love or intimacy from our mate, but we may have no idea how to get it. Or, we may just feel restless and unfulfilled, and not have any idea that our real need stems from not having enough love and intimacy with our partners. We may feel powerless in these instances, unable to trust our feelings or ourselves. And because of this, we will rarely speak up about it, and the cycle of dissatisfaction continues.

Another example many of us may face is in our workplace. If someone does something that causes us frustration, most of us are very unlikely to talk to that person about it. Instead, we complain to our co-workers, or send angry emails around. Or, we may not even be aware that that person has done something to annoy us. We may just be irritable all day, or snap at our children at dinnertime for no reason. We clamp down on our feelings, or lose touch with them completely, all in the name of being nice.

Complicity lies at the root of silence. By not speaking up—for ourselves, our families or our beliefs—we condone the way things are. In waking up to our personal stories, we begin the process of examination, which can lead to larger changes down the road. A better job is possible, which garners you more respect. More fulfilling relationships can also be achieved. More time for yourself and your hobbies, and a greater spiritual connection—all of these are possible when you connect to the power of your stories.

Our sense of connection begins with our senses. If we have kept silent, or remained complicit for any length of time, chances are that our senses, too, have shut down. Our favorite foods may not taste the same, and our favorite spring flowers may not excite us anymore. Music may not sound as moving, and we may not even notice the texture of the fabrics that lie close to our skin.

Recovering our senses is the goal for the first week of this program.

Meditation:

During the first week of this program, we will focus on re-awakening the senses. This is the first step towards waking up to our personal stories, and it's a lot harder than it sounds.

As we walk around each day, taking care of whatever business we have, we may feel as if we're able to touch, smell or taste at will. But only when we slow down enough to truly experience life do we realize that most of us have no idea how to use our sensory apparatus.

You will need a notebook and a writing implement of some kind. I do not want this to become routine or boring, so for those of you who might not think of yourselves as writers, you may choose to speak your experiences into a cassette recorder. There are many that can be had for around twenty dollars, plus the cost of tapes and batteries. More information can be found in the resources section at the back of the book, but suffice it to say that these can become very handy if the purpose of your storytelling journey is to record stories from family members and friends.

- Find a quiet place to sit, where no one will bother you for at least a half-hour. You may choose to sit on your bed, with your back against the wall, which many people with back problems report is the most comfortable and supportive posture. Others may choose to sit on a chair, or on a pillow or cushion placed on the floor, with your legs folded. There is no right way to do this, so please get comfortable. The only thing I ask is that you not recline or lie flat on your back, as this often tempts spacing out and/or falling asleep, which is not our aim here.

- Yes, I did say to find a place where no one will bother you for at least a half-hour, knowing full well that this will absolutely be the hardest part for some of you. All kinds of Parental Voices may rise up to whisper in your ear, saying, "Well, shouldn't you be watching the children, or cleaning the gutters, or getting your Ph.D. in physics? Some people are so selfish!" Of course, it's important to pay attention to your children, but as long as they are safely supervised, the other things can wait, for at least thirty minutes. Selfishness, in moderation, is an integral part of waking up to your stories.

- Now, with your eyes open or closed (it doesn't really matter, but most people find that eyes closed works best at first), begin to focus on your breathing. You may notice that the more you focus on it, the faster your heart races and the more quickly your breath moves in response. After about ten breaths, you will probably begin to notice that your heart slows down, along with your breath. Your mind, however, may be filled with racing thoughts. The mind is usually the last thing to relax.

- Take five complete breaths, trying to feel the air as it moves from the top of your chest, through your lungs as they expand, and all the way down to your belly. After you are feeling somewhat relaxed in your breathing, move your attention to your mind. Don't judge the thoughts that may be flitting through, even though the temptation will be there. "Why am I thinking about dinner?" you might wonder. Or, "I don't want to think about Maggie anymore. I'm home and my co-workers shouldn't be able to bother me here."

- When you recognize a thought occupying your mind, say "thinking," very gently, to yourself. This is a way of labeling the thought as what it is, and reminding you that it has no real power to affect you in "real" life. This is a variation on the ancient practice of shamatha vipassana meditation, meaning insight, or clear seeing. Many Buddhists and Hindus continue to practice this meditation style today. However, you do not have to espouse those beliefs to use this meditation. I use it here to begin the practice of watching our minds, which will help in waking up to our stories.

- After five minutes of this (and it will probably feel like a very long five minutes, at least at the beginning), you will probably begin to feel pretty relaxed. Your mind may still get carried away in your personal storylines, but for now, don't worry about that. Keep bringing yourself back, gently, to the present moment. Feel yourself in your body.

- Beware of the tendency to space out. This is very easy to do, because when our muscles relax, we are reminded of sleep. But this meditation is designed to help you get in touch with buried feelings, so we want to stay as alert as possible, holding an upright meditation posture without getting too rigid or too soft about it. When you feel relaxed, bring your attention to your eyes. Whether they are open or closed, think about something you saw today that had an impact on you. It may have been your child's smile, a homeless man begging for change, or the flaming red scarf around your mother's neck at lunch. Try not to overthink this. The first thought you have will probably be the one that's most meaningful. What do you notice most about this image? Is it the person's facial expression? The colors or textures? Did you notice something humorous about this image, or did it leave a lingering sense of sadness? If you are sight challenged, use your way of "seeing" as a way to experience this exercise, or use a memory of seeing. To yourself, say "seeing," and hold this image, along with the feelings it evokes, together in your mind for a few breaths. Go back to your regular meditation for one minute, allowing your mind to clear.

- Now bring your attention to your ears. Think of a sound you remember from your day today. Was it music filtering through a taxi cab radio? A dirty joke? Or was it the steady hum of the lights above you at work? Again, just let the first thing that comes to mind stay there for a bit, just resonating in your consciousness. Try to hold this image in your mind, and hear the sound as if it's present right now. Do you notice any changes in your body? A tendency to scrunch your shoulders up, or a tightening in your throat? Do you notice the desire to sing, or to offer consoling words? Let that feeling that comes along with the sound wash over you. If you are hearing challenged, use your way of "hearing" as a way to experience this exercise, or a use a memory of hearing.

  To yourself, say "hearing," and hold this image, along with the feelings it evokes, together in your mind for a few breaths. Go back to your regular meditation for one minute, allowing your mind to clear.

- Bring your attention to the skin on your hand, either on the widest part of the palm, or on the tips of the fingers. Let your mind bring forward an image of something you touched today. Maybe it was your lover's face this morning, before you left for work. Maybe it was the

Wake Up to Your Stories

smooth skin of a luscious apple, right before you bit into it. Or maybe it was the rough leather of your work boots. Just let the image of that touching come to you, along with the emotions that might have accompanied it. Did you feel tired, at being reminded of your work? Sad, at having to leave your lover behind? Or elated, because apples are by far your favorite fruit. Let the feeling and the sensation of touching co-exist in your mind for a few seconds. If there is something that prevents you from experiencing touch, use your way of "touching" as a way to experience this exercise, or use a memory of touching. To yourself, say "touching," and hold this image, along with the feelings it evokes, together in your mind for a few breaths. Go back to your regular meditation for one minute, allowing your mind to clear.

- Now bring your attention to your mouth and tongue. Really notice the feeling of your tongue in your mouth. Roll it around, letting it contact each one of your teeth. Think about the last thing you tasted, the thing that made the biggest impression on you. Maybe it was at lunch, or a snack you ate quickly in the car. If you're doing this exercise first thing in the morning, use an experience of tasting that happened yesterday, or late last night. Is it a sweet taste, like a birthday cupcake, or a rich, savory taste, like your father's signature barbecue sauce? Maybe you remember the salty flavor of chips and dip at a party. Let the taste unfold on your tongue and try to bring it forward again, if you can. Maybe your mouth will even water a little bit. And then combine this with the feeling you had during that experience. Were you terrified to turn another year older, eating that cupcake, thrilled that your father was finally going to entrust his barbecue sauce recipe to you, or nervous at making a good impression at the chip-and-dip party? Allow that feeling to exist alongside the sensation of your taste for a few breaths. If there is something that prevents you from experiencing taste, use your way of "tasting" as a way to experience this exercise, or a use a memory of tasting. To yourself, say "tasting," and hold this image, along with the feelings it evokes, together in your mind for a few breaths. Go back to your regular meditation for one minute, allowing your mind to clear.

- Now bring your attention to your nose. Try to feel the skin on your nostrils, just at the point where air starts to come inside. See if you can get in touch with the tiny hairs that filter dust out of the air for you. Slowly, allow something you smelled recently to come into your consciousness. Again, don't try to control it. Just let the first thing that comes to mind rest there for a few breaths. Maybe it's an unpleasant smell like skunk, but let it remain all the same. Try not to hold your nose. Or perhaps you smell a tub of buttery popcorn at the movies, or even a cherry pie you learned to make from a family recipe. Let the smell become tangible for you for a few breaths, and then realize the feeling you have in conjunction with this smell. Are you completely engrossed in the thriller onscreen while you eat the movie popcorn? Irritated that your dog chased a skunk again and got sprayed? Pleased that you have finally made time to bake your family this gorgeous cherry pie? Let the feeling wash over you, all the way through your body. Notices any changes that feeling brings to your body. Get as close to the smell as you can, and to the feeling that accompanies it. If there is something that prevents you from experiencing smell, use your way of "smelling" as a way to experience this exercise, or a use a memory of smelling.

To yourself, say "smelling," and hold this image, along with the feelings it evokes, together in your mind for a few breaths. Go back to your regular meditation for one minute, allowing your mind to clear.

24

- Give yourself time as you come out of the meditation. If you have had your eyes closed, open them and slowly acclimate yourself to the space around you. Approximately 15-20 minutes will probably have passed. Let yourself register how you feel after this exercise, both emotionally and physically. There are no wrong answers, and no right ones, either. Just noticing what is actually there for you will be very helpful in uncovering the stories that lie inside.

Exercise:

During the days of this week, do these meditation exercises every day. It may seem a lot in our already-crowded lives, but by the end of the week, you are likely to start noticing things about your environment, whether at school, home or work, that you have never noticed before. This is what I call the Base Practice, and you may find it useful, whenever you are feeling upset, frustrated or angry, to return to it. The Base Practice will help to open your senses again when they most want to close out any pain, anger or fear that might be surfacing in your life.

For each day of the week, pick one sense (sight, hearing, touch, taste or smell) and try to notice something about it in the course of your day. On a Hearing day, for example, I might make a special effort to tune in to the music around me, even if it's only muzak in an elevator. I might notice how the stuttering sound of a jackhammer harmonizes with the screech of a bus' brakes, or how lovely and lyrical my Jamaican neighbor's accent sounds. At first it may be hard to focus your attention this way. We are used to being buffeted with lots of information, lots of images, sounds and sometimes even tactile sensations all at once, so separating them out is one way we can start to dig out some of the unnecessary noise in our worlds.

Try to do the five sense days during the normal working

week. On the two weekend days (yes, this is homework, but it's good homework), pick two senses and try to notice two of them at the same time. It's fine if you can't do it at first. Over time, try to hold the image of a flower and the smell of truck exhaust, or the quack of a duck with the image of your grandfather's face, together in your mind. You may want to laugh about it, but you will be getting in touch with some of the absurdities we face every day, and just don't notice. Plus, it can be a fun exercise if you're feeling stale or unchallenged at work, in relationships, or in any other area of your life. Absurdity has an important function in our lives. It asks us to look beyond the surface of someone or something, in order to see the real truth that lies behind it.

Follow Up:

Using your notebook or cassette recorder, note some of the things you discovered in your meditation sessions.

- Did any images or smells pervade more than one session?

- Did any sounds, tastes or textural feelings pervade more than one session?

- Was any one sense more "awake" than the others?

- Which sense was "stretched" the most in doing these exercises?

- Did you notice a common thread among the emotions that came up?

- How were your bodily sensations affected by doing these exercises?

- Are you remembering your dreams more, or less?

- Do you find yourself anxious?

Of course, if any stories have already brought themselves to the front of your mind, make sure to record them, too. Even little memory fragments can be helpful when we want to assemble them later on. In every case, notice what happens in your emotions as well as your body when you remember these snippets of memories.

- Does your body relax with pleasure at this remembrance?

- Are your other senses activated as you pictured this person, place or thing?

- Do your shoulders tense up with anticipation?

- Is your stomach filled with butterflies?

In the next section, we will focus on the need for stories in our lives, and learn how our stories are an integral part of our spiritual, cultural and emotional development. Understanding that we are drawn to storytelling is one of the first clues that we may already be using stories in ways that do not serve us. Uncovering how stories have been traditionally used will begin to give us clues as to how we can incorporate them seamlessly into our own lives.

The Need for Stories

"All human beings have an innate need to hear and tell stories and to have a story to live by.... religion, whatever else it has done, has provided one of the main ways of meeting this abiding need."

— Harvey Cox, Professor of Divinity, Harvard

Here in the second week of our program, we will begin to think about our need for stories, and how they have shaped the universe around us, unique as it may be. First, it may be helpful to check in from last week.

- Did you do your meditation exercises every day?

- Were you able to record your experiences, both emotional and physical, using your notebook or tape recorder?

- Did you do the follow-up work on opening your senses?

- How did you find that experience? Was it stressful? Eye-opening? Hard? Easy? Relaxing?

- Did you get to do these exercises every day of the week?

- What other changes do you notice about yourself? Are you more short-tempered? Silly? Hungry? Curious?

- How has this changed your view of the future?

Tibetan Buddhists have a slogan that says, "Abandon all Hope of Fruition," which I suppose sounds a bit dire. But if we look inside that slogan, we'll see that it's really quite liberating. If we think too much about where we might end up, in relationships, with jobs or career paths, we might forget to enjoy the journey. Because my own life has had so many twists and turns, I find this slogan very helpful when working with emotions as well as stories. Stories often dictate where they want to go. Minor characters may push their way up to the front of the line and demand to be heard. What may have seemed important to you last week may seem less so now, or perhaps it has only been magnified. Being patient with that journey, instead of digging our heels in for one particular goal will help us with the next step, of recognizing our need for stories.

An Explanation of the World Around Us

As long as there has been a record of humanity, and probably even before that, there have been stories. The earliest civilizations used stories to explain the world around them, because there were no records handed down to them, no way to encompass what their experience had been like. Their stories showcased universal human concerns like food supplies, family structures and the building of communities. They spoke of threats they encountered to their security, from inclement weather or predators, or sang the praises of their providers, by detailing the number of buffalo killed during a successful hunt. Some stories closed the chapter on life, revealing a culture's burial methods and wishes for the afterlife.

The Westcar Papyrus, a document about the 4th century

Egyptian leader Khufu and his sons, is one of the earliest surviving records of storytelling. Gilgamesh, which relates the adventures of a Sumerian king, is currently thought to be the oldest surviving epic tale in Western literature.

Before stories were written down, they were drawn. Some of the earliest depictions we know of come from cave paintings found in Lascaux and Chauvet, France, which are thought to have been done in the Paleolithic Era, or Old Stone Age (30,000 BCE - 10,000 BCE). Using soil and other natural materials such as rocks and plants, painters made pigments, which have been determined, using carbon dating techniques, to be at least 18,500 years old.

In one of the caves, large red dots are painted directly onto the stone walls, along with primitive images of animals, usually horses, red deer and bears. But there are also images of rhinos, and paintings of what experts believe are leopards and hyenas, along with geometric signs arranged into panels—a series of large dots, a semicircle of smaller dots, and v-shaped bat-like symbols. Other jottings resemble insects with countless legs. In Chauvet, as many as five hundred images are crowded into these tight spaces that housed our earliest ancestors.

Other art, from the Ardeche caves like Lascaux, contain similar pigmentation patterns, and red silhouettes of human hands. Figures appear facing forward, but with their bodies in profile, which is also true of the animal depictions. Sometimes, teams of bison or ibex, all facing the same way, seem to stampede across the wall.

Most fascinating of all, though, is the fact that handprints, made by spraying or blowing pigment over the artist's hand, can be found in virtually all of the ancient caves. It's as if the people who made them were trying to cement their existence in paint, to show that they had once existed.

What scientists have not been able to sufficiently answer

is why the art was made, or what it might have meant to the inhabitants of the caves. Scholars like Marija Gimbutas point to a need for ancient peoples to measure the natural world using these symbols because they depended on hunting and growing cycles for their survival. To her, the ubiquitous dots represent the phases of the sun and moon, so crucial to the cultivation of crops. Gimbutas traces many of the other common cave symbols to the ancient goddess civilizations such as Catal Huyuk in Turkey, which used dots, spirals and chevron shapes to denote the cycles of birth, death and rebirth.

The natural ancestors of the ancient cave painters are today's mural artists. Though some have suffered derision at the hands of the traditional art establishment, which wanted nothing to do with taggers that ran afoul of the law, several of them have made powerful community art aimed at healing complex societal problems, and built bridges between seemingly disparate areas of their cities. Explaining the world around them became as necessary as breathing, so they picked up brushes and began to tell their stories.

A Way to Honor the Supernatural

Another common use of storytelling in history has been to connect with or honor the supernatural forces inherent in the world. Hurricanes, earthquakes, tornadoes and crop-killing snows have long been thought as the wrath of God or other deity. Civilizations as varied as South American corn growers and Inuit/Eskimos have offered valuable commodities such as tobacco, food, and animal pelts to the fickle gods and goddesses who seem to determine their fate on Earth.

One Inuit tale relates how the world itself came out of darkness. A woman living with her father, on her way to get water, swallows a feather, becomes pregnant, and gives birth to a baby with a raven's bill. Tulugaak (Raven) wants to play with a bladder, blown up and used to store liquids, but his mother refuses her child the toy, not wanting to anger her father. But when the baby cries inconsolably, the woman takes the bladder down off the wall. Soon, Raven's beak breaks the bladder, and light floods their home. The story ends with Raven disappearing with the dark. But light has arrived to illuminate the world.

Religions like Buddhism, Hinduism, Christianity, and Judaism have used storytelling as a way to teach moral lessons for centuries. The Hindu Ramayana, most likely composed in the 3rd century, details the adventures of Rama, who comprises one aspect of the god Vishnu. The Jakata, or birth tales, of Buddhism are often told to children to instill an early moral framework. Each tale relates a former incarnation of Gautama Buddha, and gives a teaching on the dharma, or spiritual law of Buddhism.

Christian prophets and Hasidic Jews have also used stories in their preaching, using their tales to point out wickedness, introduce rituals, or instill beliefs. Jesus, in the New Testament, uses parables, or short stories, to make his teachings more palatable to his followers. Other Bible stories are often told to children, or used during homilies to illustrate a modern issue or challenge.

Many believe that the stories from these early civilizations are the beginnings of our religious or moral lives. Oftentimes, a society's storyteller was its connection to the sacred. Since these people were trusted to remember the tribe's stories, and pass them down to subsequent generations, it was an incredibly important job, filled with responsibility and many times accompanied by ritual. Their work assured that the tribe's way of life would be preserved and respected. And most importantly, the role of storyteller assured that their way of life would continue.

A Way to Entertain Ourselves

Some cultures have used stories as a way to entertain

themselves, or to communicate their humorous experiences with other humans. Often, animals take the place of humans, enacting the embarrassing or taboo subjects. African storytellers called griots often used animals in this way because they had grown up in close proximity to wild animals, and knew their qualities well. By projecting human desires onto these animals, the griots were able to entertain the members of their tribe, and to give their people symbols that could help them cement a group identity. The tribespeople could find meaning in their everyday activities, and be reminded of the moral lesson each time they came in contact with these animals in their daily lives.

For example, the spider is a very popular symbol in African literature. Since they weave webs, spiders are thought to be very clever and hard working. In African stories, spiders are capable of overcoming obstacles and plots of all kinds, and able to connect humans to their deepest source. It is the spider who was asked to spin a thin thread that reached up to God in the sky, so all humans would have a direct path to heaven.

A Way to Gain Immortality, By Connecting with Our Ancestors

Stories have also filled a need for people to connect with the qualities or deeds of their ancestors, hoping that this would, in some way, grant them immortality. Stories derived from Spanish or Latin American cultures are especially strong when it comes to family life. In an Ecuadorian tale, an Incan King, worried about his ailing son's health and the fate of his kingdom after his own death, is told to gather some water from a magic lake at the end of the world. A golden flask is left for him to complete this task. But no one is able to find the magic lake until a young girl sets out on her pet llama. Sparrows she has previously fed with toasted corn come to her aid, fashioning a fan out of their feathers and one of her hair ribbons. The fan protects her when a crab, an alligator, and a serpent each try to keep her from her goal. One by one, the girl defeats her foes and returns to save the prince with her healing water. In return, she asks for a large farm, complete with a flock of alpaca and vicuñas, so her family will never be poor again.

A Way to Express the Beauty of Human Existence

Finally, stories have traditionally fulfilled the human need for beauty and expression. By using words, music and gestures, stories are able to show readers, listeners or viewers a glimpse of the world through the artist's eye. Ultimately, the world is reflected back to the audience member, along with a deeper understanding.

Many Asian folk tales contain moral lessons on beauty and appearance. In the story of "Jang Hwa and Hong Run," from Korea, two sisters, both beautiful and kind, live happily until their mother dies and their father remarries. Their new stepmother, who is very ugly and cruel, kills the two daughters out of jealousy. As ghosts, the two girls tell a town official what has happened, and he arrests the evil stepmother.

A traditional Korean proverb states that, "After forty years, everyone is responsible for his face," meaning that we choose whether we will live our lives in happiness or sadness, by smiling or frowning. We can control our looks, this tale seems to say, and how others perceive us.

Many other cultures have tales that include the notion that beautiful people are nice and ugly people are mean. But oftentimes, physical beauty is accompanied by beauty of spirit. Snow White cares for seven dwarves who, though hard working, are not particularly popular with the rest of the females on the planet. Cinderella is kind to animals, and recognizes the value of her ugly stepsisters as well. This quality aligns her with royalty, and allows her to attract the prince as her future husband.

We Are Our Society's Storytellers

It's easy to think about stories, because they have been with us for so long. And it's equally easy to let others be the storytellers, because we received our stories when we were most dependent on others. But as we grow and mature, it becomes our duty to remember our stories, just as it was imperative for our ancestors to remember their stories and pass them on to us. Even if we do not have a strong oral tradition in our nuclear families, we do have one as a culture. We may have formed alternative "tribes," which banded together by common religious, spiritual, political or other means. Each of these tribes has a history, or a series of stories.

Because our society is more widely diverse, and more scattered around the globe than ever before, we cannot count on just one person to carry the weight of all of our stories. Two of the most common dangers inherent in this are boredom and passivity. By sitting back and allowing ourselves to be entertained—by books, CDs, DVDs, video games, the Internet, music or other pursuits—we become passive. This does not mean that these things are bad, or that one should not use them. Instead, it's best that we engage in these activities with an awareness about them. When we listen to CDs, we may be swept away in the beauty of the music, but we do not lose touch with reality, or completely give ourselves over to the musician's power. We may play a video game and find that it increases our hand-eye coordination or improves our tennis swing. Not a bad trade-off. But in no way do we lose ourselves in the world of the game, to the detriment of our real lives.

We may say, "My life is nothing like that," when we watch a movie or look at a soap opera, but when we give up the power we have, and allow someone else to dictate our experience, we assume a kind of cultural Alzheimer's. We lose all memory for our foundations. In the most disrespectful way, we let the stories of our ancestors slip away.

Left with little or no foundation, we leave ourselves most vulnerable to others, as they rush in to fill the void. These people may be driven by pure motives, to tell meaningful or transformative stories through the media of film, television, video games, or the written word. But many are motivated purely by money, and have no real stake in whatever damage may be done to the culture as a whole. The stories they tell may be true or false, deep or shallow—it doesn't matter to them. As long as other people buy it, that is to say, allow these false stories to superimpose their own, their goals have been met.

I don't mean to suggest some sort of dark conspiracy theory of cultural rape, though this may be the end result of this type of work. Instead, the rewards are great, and there is greater temptation. Is it any wonder that something as important to cultural development as storytelling pays so well? Consciously or unconsciously, we all understand the crucial value of our stories, but may be unwilling or unable to take responsibility for the telling of them.

If we willingly give up this power, and become passive observers in our own lives, we lose the right to complain. Just as we get a vote every two years, in mid-term elections, and every four years, in presidential elections, we have the right and the responsibility to gather together and tell our stories, in large or small ways. We have been given technologies that make this more possible than ever before. Rather than letting technology divide us, with its coldness and distance, why not let it close the divide between us, or become the living symbol of interconectedness? What more proof do we need to see that stories in Kenya are as valid and important as those in Eastern Europe, Chile, and Canada?

Wake Up to Your Stories

Recovering our needs, and the needs of others, is the goal for this first week of our program. In this way, we begin to recover the needs of our families, our ancestors and the greater culture.

Meditation:

In this week's meditation, we'll get in touch with our needs. Most likely, these needs will correspond to the stories that will be most important to us. They may also come to represent the part of us that we want to work on, or re-write, using stories as the medium. You may find yourself having little moments of resistance to your meditation or follow-up exercises. That's perfectly natural. All of us are set in our ways, to a certain extent, and change does not come easy. Old patterns that may have left us without self-love are sometimes hard to break. But try to listen to the voices inside you that may be frightened this week. What do they think you might find inside yourself? Why do they not want it to come out?

- Begin by going to your private space and closing the door, making sure you will not be bothered for at least thirty minutes. This may still be hard for some of you, but I promise it will be worth your while in the long run. If nothing else, you will find yourself more relaxed and centered, but I believe you will discover a lot more than that. Take a few seconds to close your eyes and center yourself. Don't worry if your mind is very busy and active. Zen practitioners call this state "monkey mind," because thoughts flit through our minds like monkeys through trees, seemingly without grounding or direction. I like monkeys, so it doesn't bother me when my mind is all over the place. Allow your mind to just be. Notice what the thoughts are as they come and go, but don't try to chase them away.

- Give yourself five deep breaths here. When thoughts

come into your mind, label them by saying "thinking" to yourself and letting them dissolve.

- Move through each one of your senses, becoming aware of yourself as a sensory being. First feel your eyelashes, as they flutter against the rise of your cheek. If you have your eyes open for your meditation, blink your eyes a few times to give yourself a few little butterfly kisses. Focus your eyes on one thing—a wrinkle in the sheet, a carpet thread that's darker than the others—then refocus on something closer. Feel your eyes adjusting as your intention asks them to. Notice these sensations and let them go.

- Move your attention to your ears, feeling the air moving past them. Notice the subtle noises in the room— a bird flittering on the windowsill, a dull hum of an air conditioner, or steam from a radiator. Notice these sounds and let them go.

- Move your attention to your nose, feeling the tiny hairs on the inside of it as they sense new smells coming in. Notice the scents in the room, of lavender candles, unwashed feet, or home cooking from the next room. Let those smells register in your consciousness and then let them go.

- Now move your attention to your mouth and tongue. Swallow once, letting the tongue rest gently on the roof of your mouth. Notice any tastes that may be left there from your day. Is there a peppermint toothpaste aftertaste? Garlic from your lunch? Or a metallic taste from all the coffee you've been drinking? Let those tastes be in your consciousness for a few seconds, and then let them go.

- Finally, let your awareness come to the tips of your fingers, wherever they're resting. What do your fingers feel? Is it the smooth silk of your best clothes? A rough blanket? Or the leather of your office chair? Allow those sensations to occupy your attention for a few seconds, and then let them go.

- Now, that our senses are wide awake, think about your day today. What moment was the most emotionally charged for you? Did you have a fight with your co-worker about a deadline? Experience an incredible surge of love when you saw your pet running around on the lawn? Feel guilty at having missed a friend's birthday party? Hold that moment in your mind, allowing all of the emotions to flood through you. If the emotions are too intense to feel, allow them to fill up an imaginary jug beside you. What were your needs in this situation? Were they met or ignored? No matter what actually happened, what do you think you wanted out of this situation? Take five full breaths here, holding the feelings and the visual image of your emotionally loaded situation. Then go back to your regular meditation for one minute, allowing your mind to clear.

- Give yourself time as you come out of the meditation. If you have had your eyes closed, open them and slowly acclimate yourself to the space around you. Approximately 15-20 minutes will have passed. Let yourself register how you feel after this meditation. You may wish to write down your feelings in your notebook, or speak them in to your cassette recorder in order to remember them more vividly. Include descriptions of the feelings, and the situation, as much as you can. Whether speaking or writing down your experiences, remember to date them so you have a guidepost along the journey you're taking. Later on, when you refer to the notes you're taking, you may be surprised at how much has changed inside you.

Exercise:

Think about your own needs at this time of your life. Using a page in your notebook, or your cassette recorder, make a list of the needs that seem most pressing to you now. Try not to overthink it. If you can quickly come up with a list of five or so items, that's great. More is fine, too. Some prompts to get you going are:

- Your practical needs

- Your emotional needs

- Your physical needs

- Your spiritual needs

- Your mental needs

- Your familial needs

- Your educational needs

- Your nutritional needs

- Your future needs

When you are finished, look at your list. Did you write anything that's surprising to you? How does it feel to look at a laundry list of your needs? Are you ashamed? Do each of them seem like a chore to you? Or are you imbued with hope, at being able to care for yourself in this way?

Now make a list of the needs you would like to take care of soon, but in no real rush. Without thinking about it too much, just dash out a list of five or so. Separate the wishes from the needs. Your needs will be things that have an emotional tug to them, or things you cannot do without, like sleep. Wishes will be things that would feel nice, like a cashmere sweater, but are not really necessary to your survival, growth, or personal development.

Now compare these two lists. How do they match up? Is one more practical than the other? More whimsical? Is one more focused around financial security while the other is entirely about love and relationships? These lists may start to give us clues as to what's most important, storywise, for you at this time. Put these two lists aside for the moment.

Lastly, make a list of needs you may desire to fulfill, but have no idea how to get started on. You may classify these as "Long Shots," or "God Only Knows How I'm Gonna Do This" needs. Don't be shy. Be authentic. No one needs to read (or hear) these needs but you, unless you choose to share them with someone else.

Do you have an insatiable need to travel to Italy before you die? Or start your own catering business? Do you need to find the love of your life, or a perfect soulmate?

Now that you have your three lists, set them side by side, with the first list on the left, the second on the middle and the last one on the right. Assuming your normal meditation posture, look at the lists. Soften your eyes, let your mind open up a bit. Does anything on any of the lists jump out at you? Do any random thoughts or associations start to form in your mind? An example might be this. If I wrote down the need to start my own catering business, one random thought that might come into my mind is, "Maybe I can use Nana's recipes for lemon cupcakes," or "I don't have enough baking pans," or "That will never work."

It is crucial to record any feelings or seemingly random thoughts that come up at this time. Allowing ourselves to relax into the meditation posture in this way can often open our minds to little clues about what our minds may be trying to tell us under the surface. Don't try to make sense of these thoughts or associations now. Just write them down in your notebook or speak them into your tape recorder. They will find their way into your stories, or at least point you in the right direction. Each of us is unique and different, and only you will be able to use your unique guideposts to travel your path.

Follow-Up:

This week, I'd like you to continue doing the Base Practice

every day, ideally for fifteen minutes or more. The process of relaxation, both in ourselves and as we relate to the outside world, is very important, as is the process of awakening our senses. Try something new this week. Get a weird new fruit from the grocery store, or buy an especially comfortable pair of socks (maybe even cashmere!).

For each day of this week, notice a need that comes up for you. It may be as simple as a feeling of thirst and then taking a drink of water. Each day, write or speak the need that came up, and the action you took in trying to meet it. You may not succeed in meeting every need that comes up. Some are a lot larger than others, so please do not be hard on yourself. The purpose of this exercise is to become increasingly aware of our needs, so that we can set a course toward changing things that do not currently satisfy us. You may even wish to write in your notebook how you would like the need to be met in the future. Remember, we cannot control how other people respond to us, but we can control how we decide to feel about it. Be realistic, but balance your realism with your playful side.

Now comes the hard part. In thinking about our needs and the process of meeting them, I would like you to start thinking about the needs of others. This may be a loaded issue for some. We may feel as if we go out of our way to meet others' needs, only to have ours ignored, or that we care for children, our bosses, our spouses, our parents, our communities, etc., almost to the point of exhaustion.

This exercise is not meant to deepen a sense of mental or emotional fatigue. But every coin has its flip side. Our needs can only be considered when others feel heard and seen and fulfilled, perhaps by us. Trying to get our needs met from people who are as stretched thin as we are is often an exercise in futility. So this week, pick one person. I'll let you be the judge, but I find that this practice works well with someone we normally feel neutral about, but who sometimes has the power to irritate us or get under our skin. Focus on this person at least once during the week. What needs does this person seem to broadcast when he or she is speaking or acting? Is this person direct enough to ask for help in meeting these needs? Or do you notice ways in which this person is afraid of asking for what they truly want? How does the person hold their body when they're at their most vulnerable?

You do not need to confront this person about your observations or feelings about them. But you may wish to make notes in your notebook about what you've discovered, along with any changes you notice in your emotions and body.

There are two additional parts of this practice. One is to give something to this person during the week. It does not need to be a piece of tangible property, but it can be. For instance, you may notice that someone you know needs a ride, and it's raining outside. Extend the offer, even if it might cause you to lose the ten minutes of pure "you" time you have per day. Maybe the receptionist at work has gotten swamped with work. On your lunch break, you might offer to bring her back something from the deli and not ask for payment in return. The really fulfilling times, for me, are when I find myself giving a teeny bit beyond what I'm normally comfortable with. This is the point that I notice things about myself and my own needs.

The second aspect of the practice is to notice what you share with this person. You may feel about as far away in ethnic background, cultural practices, or economic circumstances as could be. But there is something that connects you to this person, even if it's just the fact that you're both human and you both have needs. Write or speak about your observations. Allow these common threads to exist in your mind for a few minutes.

It would be great to try a new person to practice with for

each day of the week. If you don't feel up to that, just one person on one day of the week will give you the full benefit. Next week, we'll focus on what our stories mean to us, and how we find meaning in our day-to-day lives. As we begin to see not only our need for stories, but also a way to use them in the concrete sense, we begin to open our hearts to the idea that our stories, equally valuable, can occupy a space in the pantheon of human experience.

3 *What Our Stories Mean*

"A child... who has learned from fairy stories to believe that what at first seemed a repulsive, threatening figure can magically change into a most helpful friend is ready to believe that a strange child whom he meets and fears may also be changed from a menace into a desirable companion."

— Bruno Bettelheim

At this point, we've completed the first two weeks of the program, and you may have begun to notice certain changes taking place inside you. You may have started to notice more external events with your senses, or you may find that your goals and priorities have shifted, even if it's just a little bit. In this third week, we'll begin to think about how our stories might be used in our everyday, contemporary lives. On most days, while we're rushing around trying to meet deadlines, take care of children, or advance our goals and aspirations, the concept of storytelling might seem somewhat less important than getting one's practical needs met. But as we saw in last week's exercise, our needs may be anything but practical. Writing and sharing stories is one very valuable way to change the reality around you. Only in understanding the past can we hope to change the future.

Let's take a moment to check in from last week:

- Did you have a chance to do the meditation exercises every day?

- Did you do the follow-up work, by making lists of your needs?

- What did you find out about yourself when you compared these lists?

- How were your emotions affected by doing this exercise? What emotions came up most prevalently for you?

- Were you able to work on noticing another person's needs?

- How frequently did you do these exercises? With how many people?

- What was your emotional experience of this practice with someone else?

- What changes did you notice about yourself when you gave something to this person? Were you surprised by your reaction, or did you expect it?

- How has this changed your view of what might be possible in the future?

Before reading this chapter, take a minute to check in with yourself. How are you feeling, both emotionally and physically? Do you notice any resistance in your body? If you have one strong or prevailing emotion, ask yourself what that might be about. Listen closely. Your body may tell you that it needs more—more sleep, water, nutrients, vitamins, love, or protection. It's important, while undertaking this process, to make sure your physical body, which is undergoing changes all the time, is not left out in the cold while we do our mental and emotional work.

Using Our Stories

Now that we've looked into the history of storytelling a bit, and learned the five major ways they have been used throughout history, we can start to think about how our stories affect our daily lives.

Most of us make up stories in our minds all the time, though these may remain unconscious. We may meet a guy at a party and before we've even had dinner together, we've already seen ourselves on our fourth, fifth and tenth dates. We've picked out our silverware patterns, our wedding dress, and the place we'll spend our honeymoons. I call this process Unconscious Storytelling, because we do it all the time, usually without noticing it. We are so used to hearing stories, and waiting for the "happily ever after" ending, that we script it into our own lives all the time.

This is great, on one level. It gives us events to look forward to, provides us impetus for achieving goals, and allows us little flights of fancy, in which a creative world, where anything is possible, exists. It has been posited that this is why we dream. But there are times when Unconscious Storytelling is not healthy. Rather than allowing us to remain open to a moment as it happens, our minds may whirl us off in any direction that seems more entertaining or fantastical. Crushing disappointment comes when we find that the reality of a given situation doesn't match up with what's in our minds. This can lead to depression, anxiety and suicidal feelings.

Here I need to add a disclaimer. This book is not meant to take the place of professional mental health care. If you have a history with depression or anxiety, please undertake these exercises under the guidance of your healthcare practitioner. If you find yourself experiencing painful memories, please stop doing these exercises and talk to a counselor or therapist. The purpose of this book is not served by burdening you with unbearable pain. We may all experience twinges of sadness, as well as other emotions, in waking up to our stories. But there is no shame in asking for help, if this is what you truly need.

Healing from Abuse or Neglect

This may be especially true when dealing with a past that may include abuse and neglect. Abuse does not have to be extreme—beatings or sexual abuse, for example— to be felt deeply and remembered by the tissues of the body. Being yelled at, undermined, second-guessed, or even ignored can leave lasting scars that are frequently buried as the mind seeks to help us survive. Some of these scars can be healed through writing down and sharing our stories with others. Bearing witness to pain and suffering, whether borne by us or someone else, is a way of closing the circle on the past, and declaring that it does not have the power to hurt us anymore.

A woman I will call Clara decided to leave her abusive husband in the middle of the night, with her two children in tow. With little money and unreliable transportation, she made her way from Alaska down to Seattle in the middle of a rainstorm. Though she was terrified, she did not want to let on to her children. Her wish was that they would grow up in a household where fear was not their primary emotion. When she shared the story of her escape, which she chose to write in a notebook with the help of a therapist, the rest of our story group's members wept quietly, or extended their arms to her in a hug. When she was done, she put her head down. We all gave her a minute, thinking she needed to compose herself. But when she looked up, she was beaming from ear to ear, at finally being able to release her pain.

Connecting with Relatives and Family Members

Connecting with relatives and family members can seem daunting, if we don't happen to come from a close family. If we have been adopted, this may seem even more impossible. And if a parent or beloved family member has died, we may have given up trying to communicate with this person.

Sometimes, collecting our family stories allows us to have a sense of where we've come from. Humorous stories about missed connections or nervous wedding dances can take their place in our mental scrapbook, alongside recipes from our grandmothers, and pictures of proud immigrants entering Ellis Island.

But getting family members to share their stories may be another matter entirely. For years, whenever my family gets together, I have tried to get my grandmother to talk about how her life used to be. I ask about the buildings downtown, how the town has changed since she was a child, and where she met my grandfather. I ask about what she studied in college, an unusual path for a woman of her time.

Mostly, she clams up, or says she can't remember. And I would be happy to let her off the hook if she didn't have the uncanny habit of remembering the answers to my questions when I'm pulling on my coat to leave. It's almost as if she doesn't want to tell me her stories, though I don't think she's consciously withholding them from me. I tried to get sneaky once, and placed a recorder behind the couch, where she couldn't see it. All I got were muffled voices and the sound of people shifting their weight.

You may have similar experiences, begging your parents or grandparents to share their experiences. Of course, you can ask politely, or even make it easier for them to tell their stories by recording them, but none of us can force them to share. Even if we're polite, we may continue to encounter silence, indifference, or even anger. Most people don't believe that others will care if they tell their stories—it's the way that most of us have been raised. Still, there may be a way to get access to these stories, even if the other person doesn't want to share them.

On birthdays or at Christmas time, ask your parent or grandparent to give you something of theirs, such as a medal won in a high school track meet, a picture taken during a flirtation with photography, or a musical instrument they no longer play. When you receive the gift, ask them to tell you the story behind the object, with all the details they can remember. If their memory seems to stumble (let's face it, we all forget sometimes), come prepared with a series of leading questions to help them along. Gentle nudges like, "When did you start playing this instrument?" or "Were you in the band for all four years of high school?" or "Who was your best friend at the time?" all show that you are really interested, not just being polite.

On my last birthday, my grandmother sent a blue velvet jewelry box with a charm bracelet inside. It was a heavy gold link chain, like they used to wear in the forties and fifties, and there was one charm on it, a medal that said "Oratory." Now I have always wanted to write, ever since I was a child, and have always felt like an outsider in my family, since no one else shares this burning desire. I called my mom and said, "Gram sent me a charm bracelet with an oratory charm. I didn't know she had done public speaking."

"No," my mother told me. "That's mine. I won that in grade school, in a contest. My speech was on the poem inscribed on the Statue of Liberty. I can still remember it, word for word."

As she rattled off the poem, I bent over to retrieve my jaw from the floor. I had lived with my mother for many years, yet no one had ever told me that she had won a public speaking contest, and had wanted to write and act (two things I had already manifested signs of, in copious school plays, poems, and short stories). My own need to tell stories didn't seem so "outsider" to me then. She even found the powder-blue typewriter she had used to type her speech, which I proudly display in my office.

To Leave Something Behind

If we have children or grandchildren, or are planning to have children, we will most likely want to have a record of our family life, to leave something behind for them. Before "scrapbooking" became a verb, people kept scrapbooks filled with photos, captions, napkins from fancy restaurants, dried flowers, and even report cards, pressed between the leaves of the album. These were passed down, generation to generation, leaving behind a record of the relative's existence. Little clues could be found in these pages, at how life was for the people who had made it possible for us to exist. In keeping these albums, we agreed not to forget our ancestors, and the lives they had arranged so that we could be more comfortable. Using these keepsakes, we are able to draw closer to people we may never even have known.

We may see our nose on the face of an uncle long departed, or a squinted gesture our own child shares with the grandmother he will never meet. Gathering stories to go with our pictures can only deepen this experience of connection, with our roots, our families, and the forces that came together to create us.

Some of us may share traditions of storytelling whenever our families meet, for holidays, in celebration, or even when one of our tribe passes on. If so, waking up to these stories may add value and depth to our search for meaning. For example, there may be an often-repeated story that features a rather indelicate tumble involving us, a plate of potato salad, and the family dog. While the tale may be told in a light-hearted spirit, allowing this story to be repeated may make it true on some level. Though we may not be clumsy at all, and instead just fell that one time because the grass was slippery, or we were wearing new shoes for the occasion, if we allow these stories to exist unchallenged, we consent to their becoming our history.

We'll talk more about rewriting our stories in Chapter 9, but suffice it to say that in order to leave something behind for others, we must make sure that the record we're leaving is accurate, and not just something that has been repeated so often it just feels that way.

To Express Ourselves and the World We Live In

One of the most popular uses of storytelling has always been to entertain. When we want a child to go to bed, we tell tales that will distract her from the monsters allegedly living in the closet. When we want to impress a potential new mate, we share stories of our youth, sometimes flirting with the urge to embellish our accomplishments ever so slightly. Underneath these is the desire to entertain.

Entertainment is a valuable use of storytelling today as well. When we are feeling bored, a story filled with action and adventure can motivate us to become more engaged with our own lives. Similarly, if we are living through a personal crisis, stories of others going though struggles like our own can make us feel that much less alone in the universe.

When we really want to entertain someone else with our stories (and it doesn't matter whether the story is happy, sad, inspirational, or depressing as all hell), we are showing them that we care. Taking the time to make the connection with someone else through stories is a way of establishing a shared humanity. A story may take us in the opposite direction from our current concerns and become a learning experience, about another culture, another country, or a different perspective, skewed slightly from our own. When we share our stories with other people with the intention to entertain, we are saying, "I see you. You exist. And I want to communicate with you alone."

To Become More Visible

With that being said, there are many groups of people that have been traditionally ignored by the prevailing stories, or at least the ones that have made history. These are sometimes the most interesting, at least to me, because there is often a reason they have been left out of history. They are too threatening, too controversial, or too achingly human.

Though most cultures have rich and varied storytelling traditions, few of them have had the visibility available to most white European cultures. African and slave tales, though absorbed into American storytelling cycles like the Uncle Remus books, were largely viewed as primitive or sub-literate. American television and movies, as extensions of this tradition, relegated non-white actors and actresses to roles like maids, manicurists and gardeners, depending on their ethnicity. Only on shows like Star Trek could someone see a racially-integrated cast interacting in a color blind society, perhaps because it was supposed to have taken place in the distant future!

In the 1980s, that began to change. Television had The Cosby Show and the movies had Eddie Murphy. Rising stars like Denzel Washington, Jennifer Lopez and Chow Yun-Fat began to appear on our cultural radar. In the literary world, Walter Mosely, Amy Tan, and Gabriel Garcia Marquez enthralled us with their words.

Visibility remains one of the primary uses of storytelling today because it breaks down barriers. People who might be sympathetic to your cause but might not know how to help can find out, second-hand, what it feels like to be inside your skin. People who may not be sympathetic, or even interested, cannot help but respect, or at least notice you for who you are. Ultimately, we may not even tell our stories for others, but to prove to ourselves that we are here, and that we have something to say about our experience.

To Ensure That Our Way of Life Continues

Finally, we share our stories to help others remember us. Even if we have been driven out of our families, or distanced from our cultures by expatriation, or written out of the family will, chances are we have created a life that we want to continue after we have left the planet. We have discussed the sense of relief that comes with leaving something behind for our children, but waking up to our stories can also be a powerful way to make sure that the lives we have so carefully created for ourselves and our families can continue. Family traditions, religious or cultural customs, or even patterns of speech can be preserved in stories almost as if the person in them were still alive. In this way, we cheat death, and keep our loved ones alive in spirit.

Our personal stories can also bring us a good deal of money. If our lives have been particularly interesting, inspired or strange, and we're willing to do the work to write these stories down, we can go the traditional publishing route, by selling our stories to literary magazines or publishers (if they can be collected in book form). We can also choose to self-publish our stories, for distribution to our friends and family members at holidays. More on this can be found in Chapter 11, Taking It Further.

For now, though, we'll focus on the process of waking up to our stories, and giving ourselves the green light to speak them out loud. In time, we may find it possible to write ourselves out of "stuck" places or dead-end jobs, and into satisfying relationships and careers. By establishing firm intentions, we remove any potentially airy-fairy aspect of this process. Let me tell you, there is nothing magic about it. When we look at our lives full in the face, and are willing to make changes to whatever we don't like, we have made an agreement to become an active participant in our own lives, and in our culture at large. On any given day, this will trump the starry-eyed fantasist in all of us.

Meditation:

For this week's meditation, we're going to get in touch with the way we use our stories in our daily lives. Though we may feel as if we know ourselves, or have a pretty good idea of how we "talk to ourselves," opening up to our stories in this way will help us realize the ways in which we might need to do some rewriting.

As we move through this meditation, think about ways you may be judging yourself. These may take the form of tiny instances, or fractions of seconds. You may speak harshly to yourself in your mind, saying, "THINKING!" as if you are speaking to a bad puppy. "BAD Meditator," you may say to yourself. That is not the point of this exercise. For now, just noticing these little instances is wonderful. Over the next few weeks, we will work on letting those harsh voices go, in order to replace them with gentler and more accepting ones.

How are you seeing yourself this week? And how do you communicate with that "self" you see? Do you find yourself afraid to show "the real you," for fear that no one will understand or appreciate it?

- Begin by going into the place you will be doing your meditation, and make sure that no one will disturb you for at least twenty minutes. Allow yourself to come into your meditation posture in as relaxed a way as you can. Rather than forcing your body into this rigid position, try finding it naturally, feeling your way along with your body. A wonderful instruction I received came from a teacher who urged us to feel as if we were being held upright by a string attached to the top of our heads. That way, it may be easier to come into an upright but relaxed position.

- Close your eyes and take a few breaths here, letting all the thoughts from your day empty out. If some thoughts remain, or will not leave, let that be. I find that my mind is different all the time. Even on days I feel completely calm and rested, my mind may race around like a lunatic. So if you find yourself becoming impatient, try to remember that your mind is part of you. It houses important parts of your being, including your facilities with language and memory. As such, it is the seat of your stories. Your mind is busy all day helping you accomplish all kinds of tasks. Give it some slack.

- Let your breathing slow down, taking five or six deep breaths. Feel the oxygen as it enters the top part of your lungs at your breastbone, all the way down to your stomach and belly. If your eyes are open, watch your belly rise with the nourishing breath, so crucial to keeping you alive. Don't worry, no one's watching. Let your belly be full and round.

- As thoughts come into your mind, label them by saying "thinking" to yourself. Usually, the thoughts will be released this way. If not, keep reminding yourself gently that these are creations of your mind, not concrete events. It is not a goal to get rid of your thoughts or feelings here, rather to see them accurately as they move through your mind.

- Move through your senses, using a different order this week. Begin to become aware of the sounds in the room, however faint. Maybe you can hear a couple arguing next door, or the hammering of a plumber on the pipes. Maybe your cat is distracting you, and purring as she winds herself around your legs. Notice the way you feel about each sound, and how that feeling lodges in the tissues of your body. If you have an intense reaction, like anger or frustration, try to re-adjust your body so that you are balanced and relaxed again.

- Now notice the smells in the room. One by one, let them float past your consciousness. The laundry detergent rising from a stack of freshly-washed clothes, lavender bath beads, or your sweat from a recent run. Label these sensory experiences and let them go.

- Bring your attention to your skin. Try not to think about it too much, just wherever your attention moves to first. Is the sensation dry? Tight? Relaxed and loose? Notice the way your skin is registering information about the room itself. Is it too warm or too cold? Are you itchy?

- Your tongue is the seat of taste in your body, so move your attention there for a moment. Notice how your tongue is affected when you're actually thinking about it. Most times, we move through our day without really noticing what the tongue is doing for us, or how it is affected by what we do, unless we burn ourselves or bite the tongue by mistake. Feel the tongue in your mouth. Move it around for a few seconds. There is a great yoga pose called Lion Pose that's very silly, but liberating. From your meditation position, sit upright and open your jaw as wide as possible, sticking out your tongue as far and down as it will go. Keep your gaze on the tip of your nose. This pose is said to resemble the lion's roar, and is the "destroyer of all diseases."

- Now let's check in with your eyes. If they are open as you sit in meditation, let them close. Do you see any colors behind your eyes? Or a thin thread of light as your eyelids shut out the room? If your eyes are already closed, open them, registering how the incoming light affects what you see. If you narrow your eyes slightly, how do the images around you shift?

- When you are finished awakening your senses, let your mind move through the events of your day or, if you're doing this practice in the morning, thinking about the events of last night, or yesterday. What storylines did you find yourself taking part in? Were any of them Unconscious Storytelling? For example, when your friend didn't call you at the right time, did your mind spin a tale worthy of Moby Dick? Notice which direction your storyline took you. Did you panic, and worry that she had been kidnapped or killed? Did you assume that she liked another friend better, and was on the phone with that person right now, talking about you? The way we construct our moment-to-moment stories can shed light on the way we're currently talking to ourselves.

- Let that storyline unfold in your mind, taking five slow, deep breaths. If the memory of this event is traumatic, allow yourself to stay with it as long as possible. You may find yourself wanting to replay the incident again and again, or talk back to the person in your mind, arguing with her as if she's standing right next to you. Try not to let yourself "spin out." By this I mean don't try to hurt yourself again, by replaying it over and over. Instead, try to use the tools you have been working with so far to redirect your attention. If you need to, stop thinking about this event altogether, and return to watching your mind, saying "thinking" to yourself whenever you notice a thought in your mind.

- Now that we have an idea of how we might have gotten caught up in a storyline of some sort, let's think about what we wanted to get out of the situation. Whenever we engage with another person, chances are we want something. It may not be as crass as all that. We all go to work not because we are trying to manipulate someone but because we need money to pay our rent and bills. Spend a few breaths thinking about what you wanted to achieve by this interaction. If it does not come to you immediately, don't worry about it. Keep doing the Base Practice. Some people spend their entire lifetimes trying to figure themselves out, so it's not important that we do it in one night, or three weeks. The point is to try to connect our needs, which we focused on last week, with the way we use our stories in our everyday lives. So for example, you may find that you engaged with this person for one of the reasons above, to entertain perhaps, or to make sure your quality of life was maintained.

- Lastly, think about how your needs or desires, combined with the storyline you created, made you feel. Try not to be ashamed if you felt like you lost a little control. We all do it, so there is no shame at all. Every living person, at some time, gets caught up in the details of life so much that everything else, even important people and goals, fade into the background. How did you end up feeling about yourself? Are you still feeling that way now?

- Take five full breaths here, letting your personal storyline and the feelings associated with it dissolve. As part of the past, it has no ability to hurt you anymore, even if you have to see that person tomorrow. Then go back to your regular meditation for one minute, allowing your mind to clear.

Exercise:

When you come out of your meditation, please record the storyline you found yourself engaging in, and how it made you feel, especially about yourself. Note any changes you noticed in your body as well. Date the entry, whether you were writing or speaking it.

Next, review the five main ways we use stories in our everyday lives:

- Healing from Abuse or Neglect
- Connecting with Relatives and Family Members
- To Leave Something Behind
- To Express Ourselves and the World We Live In
- To Become More Visible
- To Ensure That Our Way of Life Continues

Which one appeals to you the most? Without thinking twice about it, which one jumps out at you? Right that one down in your notebook, or speak it into your recorder. Once you have identified the main reason you are attracted to stories and storytelling, notice if anything else jumps into your mind right after that. If so, note it down, too.

Now that you have been training your mind for a few weeks, you may have begun to notice that your thoughts are no longer just flying around unnoticed. You may even be able to laugh at some of the things you find yourself thinking, seemingly without your permission. Any thought you have immediately following one of your meditation sessions is likely to be very revealing about who you are, and the sometimes hidden goals and agendas you may be carrying along with you.

So try to notice the feelings you have when you decide you want to tell stories. Even though you presumably bought this book (or someone lent it to you) and you have been dutifully carrying out these practices for three weeks, I am continually surprised by the fact that it takes people awhile to admit that they actually want to tell stories. After you have identified the way you want to use stories in your life right now (you can always choose another method later on), please take a moment to sit with that, giving yourself

60

permission to undertake this work because you find it necessary.

If not, just record any random thoughts, feelings or story fragments as they come to you. Pat yourself on the back for making it almost a third of the way through this process. You are doing great work for yourself, and may have already started to reap the emotional rewards.

Follow-Up:

This week, please continue with the Base Practice every day. But try to steal a few more minutes from your day. Twenty-five minutes would be great, but if not, try for twenty-one instead of twenty. Showing yourself, in real terms, that you are willing and able to take care of yourself will slowly start to change old patterns of accepting less from the world.

For each day of this week, notice one storyline that you get caught up in. This can be internal or external. An internal example might be making up our minds about someone before we've even talked to him for five minutes. An external example would be becoming overly involved in office politics, or forming hardcore opinions about these events when they don't really concern us personally.

Take some time to record the storyline you have identified, as well as its emotional effects on you. Please resist the temptation to be hard on yourself. There is no right way to go through this, and no wrong way. There is only looking at what is, and dealing with that in an accepting manner.

The purpose of this exercise is to start waking up to the myriad ways we use stories in our day-to-day lives. Please make sure to accompany your storylines with all the feelings that may have been running through your head when it happened, as well as the feelings associated with telling this story, even to a notebook or recording device.

The challenging part of this follow-up, for those who want to try it, is to attempt to notice yourself becoming involved in a storyline either as it's happening, or before it even gets a chance to pull you in. It's not a race or a contest, so it's no big deal if this doesn't happen this week. Remember that this is a process, and any progress at all is really helpful. If you find yourself feeling "hooked," as Buddhist teacher Pema Chodron so cogently puts it, try to find a way to wriggle off the hook. You might say to yourself "thinking," putting this storyline in the same category as any random thought that comes up in your meditation practice. Or you may choose to be more practical about it.

For instance, if you are about to lose your patience with your spouse or child, look at that raw edge you find yourself up against. How sensitive we can all be, and how alike one another. Another of Pema Chodron's teachings is very helpful in these situations. To myself I say, "Just like me," while thinking about the irksome person or situation, and sometimes even while looking directly at the person. Even if it's done through gritted teeth (everyone does that, too, so don't worry about it), it's really hard not to see our shared and very fallible human nature in those moments. Usually, the heat behind the emotion you're carrying will dissipate, and it will be possible to redirect the storyline to a more fruitful outcome.

Whether you choose to try this last part of the practice or not, write down or speak about your experiences. See how each of us shares a common thread, of internal and external storytelling, whether we're using these stories constructively or not. Allow a deeper understanding of this fundamental interconnectedness to permeate your consciousness.

Next week, we'll focus on what stands in the way of us sharing our stories, and how we can shift the dynamic to allow us greater access to them. Waking up to our stories depends on our ability to get in touch with our obstacles, and

Wake Up to Your Stories

the subtle ways in which we allow them to stay in place. And along the way, we may discover that we needn't remove or destroy them, but merely adopt a posture of compromise.

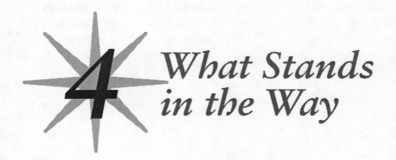

What Stands in the Way

"All my stories are about the action of grace on a character who is not very willing to support it, but most people think of these stories as hard, hopeless and brutal."

— Flannery O'Connor

After three weeks of engaging with the process of waking up to your stories, you may have begun to feel like an antenna, picking up little nuances in relationships, and even in your own emotional landscape. You may have sensory experiences that are more vivid than before you started the program, and notice that part of you may have been on auto-pilot in your major relationships. As you continue the program, you may become more devoted than ever to caring for yourself, or decide to make a conscious shift in your long-term goals. This is all very normal.

As we open up to our needs, and the uses of our stories, it's inevitable that we begin to change somehow. I know that even the word change can make people tense up slightly, or flip out entirely. I'll be happy to substitute transformation instead, if it will make you feel better. The important core of this process is to understand that change is not a bad word. You can welcome change as a sign of energetic movement around the things you want to transform (that word again!) in your own life.

There's a flip side, too. Some people think that in order to have the lives they want, they just need to tweak the variables they want to adjust, like dialing a thermostat from 68 to 70 degrees. But this is rarely the way life works. Instead, the tiniest parts of our lives are not only interconnected, but interdependent. We cannot get a job unless we have a resume. We cannot construct a resume if we don't have good work experience. And rarely do we have good work experience if we do not have a healthy self-image.

Uncovering the uses of our stories, as we did last week, begins the process of noticing how we are already using stories, or allowing ourselves to be used in stories. In this fourth week, we'll begin to get in touch with what commonly stands in the way. As you might have noticed in the follow-up exercises last week, our personal storylines can completely carry us away, until we move from the driver's seat into the passenger seat, giving up our power and allowing ourselves to stop developing on the spot. Being aware enough to notice our stories, along with what stands in the way, is one step closer towards changing patterns that no longer serve our growth.

Think about your week last week:

- Did you get to do your meditation exercises every day?
- Did you do the follow-up work, noticing the storylines in your everyday life?
- Did you notice any particular emotion dominating your thoughts?

- If so, how did having that emotion make you feel about yourself?

- Were you able to take this a step further and notice how others may be including you in their stories?

- Did you try to stop a storyline before it carried you off into old and familiar behavior patterns?

- If so, what were the results?

- Finally, were you surprised at the results of these practices, or did they seem very normal and expected?

Before starting a new week of waking up to your stories, take a minute to check in with yourself. Notice any feelings of trepidation, fear or tension in your body. How are you feeling emotionally? Is anything weighing especially heavily on your mind? If so, note it down in your notebook, or speak it into your recorder. Allow the way things are to be all right with you.

Challenges

When I first began to work with people and their stories, about twelve years ago, I was surprised by the response I got. People of all kinds wanted to wake up to their stories, and to have a platform from which to tell them. But when I asked if they had any challenges to getting in touch with their stories, most of them responded negatively.

When we began to do the exercises, though, many people began to experience fear. I suppose I could have blamed myself, wondering if I had given them these fears. But when I asked a series of targeted questions, I realized that the workshop participants had been viewing the word stories to mean only the anecdotes they told at parties, usually to break the ice or get a laugh.

"No one is afraid of that," I said to them.

"We know. That's why we said we couldn't think of any challenges when you asked us."

A bell in my head went off – bing!

"What if I rephrase the question? When you want to tell a story that's longer or more serious than stories you'd tell at a party, what makes you feel bad about the process?"

Several hands shot up around the room.

"I never have the time I need to write them down."

"No one wants to listen to what I say."

" Yeah, I mean, why should anyone care what's happened to me?"

"I can barely spell. I'm not good enough to be a writer."

"My dad is a great storyteller, but I'm not that great."

"I'm way too shy to tell stories in front of other people. They might laugh."

"Maybe I'll hurt someone's feelings."

"Or maybe it didn't really happen that way. Maybe I'm the only one who remembers it like that."

"I don't have plans to publish my stories, so why tell them?"

"Ok," I said. "Anyone else want to make a comment?"

One last hand went up, a little tentatively.

"I don't know how to put it. I just don't know if I have the right to tell these stories. They're personal, and they're mine."

"You mean you don't want to share them with others? That's okay. You don't have to say them out loud if you don't want to."

"No, I just don't know if I can …"

Maybe one of these sounds very familiar to you. Maybe you picked up this book, or had someone lend it to you, and you had every intention of reading it. Maybe you've gotten this far in the program, diligently doing your meditations and follow-up exercises. But some part of you isn't completely committed to the idea that waking up to your personal stories can be beneficial to you in your practical, day-to-day life. That very feeling may be one of the ways you are unconsciously sabotaging yourself from achieving the very things your mind tells you you want to achieve. Waking up to the way you use stories in your life provides a very powerful weapon to smash these little ways we all have of sabotaging the things we claim to want for ourselves.

Lack of Time

Since the 1980s, when the world seemed to accelerate, a climate of busyness has descended on our culture. Devices designed to make our lives easier, like cell phones, computers, and Blackberries can also make it harder. By bringing so much information directly to our doorsteps and desktops, we are confronted with an intimidating amount of pressure to read more, react more, and communicate more. This can often push us beyond our comfort zone. It can transgress our boundaries, and force us to become more vigilant than ever about reinforcing them. And it can make us believe that there will never be enough time to do it all.

In a climate like this, focusing on oneself can seem frivolous. We may feel that there are more important things to do than dredging up stories from our past. We may even label ourselves selfish for wanting to delve more deeply into our psyches.

Since time has become such a commodity in our culture, it has also been made more valuable. If someone is busy, he or she is considered important. We tiptoe around that person as if they could be easily broken by our requests for attention or companionship. We talk about squeezing someone into our schedule, as if that person is as malleable as rubber.

But none of us really is that malleable. We are fragile, fallible beings. We need love and attention, not a slot on someone's calendar. So in a certain way, making time for people is a revolutionary act of protest. By recognizing the importance of friendship and bonding, not above but alongside family and love relationships, we make a courageous stand for humanity.

I love computers as much as the next person. They make it easy to store and remember data. But I do not mistake my computer for my boss, or as something that will control the way I live my life. I do not try to use my computer in place of a friend. Same for the cell phone and Blackberry.

We all have responsibilities that go along with our jobs. But telling ourselves that it's all right to unplug from this grid may be more convincing if it's related to our health. According to a recent study by the National Institute for Occupational Safety and Health:

- 38% of women and 26% of men report that they feel "time-stressed."

- 40% of workers reported their job was very or extremely stressful.

- 25% view their jobs as the number one stressor in their lives.

- 75% of employees believe that workers have more job stress than 10 years ago.

- 29% of workers felt quite a bit or extremely stressed at work.

- 26% of workers said they were "often or very often burned out or stressed by their work."

- Job stress is more strongly associated with health complaints than financial or family problems.

- 62% routinely find that they end the day with work-related neck pain.

- 44% reported stressed-out eyes.

- 38% complained of hurting hands.

- 34% reported difficulty in sleeping because they were too stressed-out.

- 30% suffered from back pain.

- 28% complained of "stress."

- 20% reported feeling fatigued.

- 17% reported having muscular pains.

- 13% had headaches.

Another study, done by the Centers for Disease Control, found that:

- Stress is linked to physical and mental health, as well as decreased willingness to take on new and creative endeavors.

- Repetitive musculoskeletal injuries, such as carpal tunnel syndrome, have become the nation's leading workplace health cost, and account for almost a third of all Workers' Compensation awards.

- Job burnout experienced by 25% to 40% of U.S. workers is blamed on stress.

- More than ever before, employee stress is being recognized as a major drain on corporate productivity and competitiveness.

- Depression, only one type of stress reaction, is predicted to be the leading occupational disease of the 21st century,

Wake Up to Your Stories

responsible for more working days lost than any other single factor.

- $300 billion, or $7,500 per employee, is spent annually in the U.S. on stress-related compensation claims, reduced productivity, absenteeism, health insurance costs, direct medical expenses (nearly 50% higher for workers who report stress), and employee turnover.

- Women who work full-time and have children under the age of 13 report the greatest stress worldwide.

- Nearly one in four mothers who work full-time and have children under 13 feel stress almost every day.

- Globally, 23% of women executives and professionals, and 19% of their male peers, say they feel "super-stressed."

- Stress is linked to the six leading causes of death, heart disease, cancer, lung ailments, accidents, cirrhosis of the liver, and suicide.

Kind of makes you think, doesn't it?

The irony is this: we want to make changes to our lives so that we can get out of the rat race, but sometimes, we find ourselves unwilling or unable to make the very changes that we need to make in order to facilitate this process. When you look at it that way, there is only one answer, and that is to make changes that allow us more time for ourselves, until the time spent working is balanced with time spent on the other aspects of our lives. Waking up to our stories is one way we can do this.

We Don't Feel Qualified to Write

Another common challenge is that many of us don't feel qualified to tell our stories. I don't know if it's a function of our school system or something else entirely, but if we don't consider ourselves good spellers, we don't consider ourselves worthy of writing. Somehow, we expect our first drafts to be Shakespeare-worthy, or capable of landing us a National Book Award.

It's always great to set high standards. Usually, it makes us strive to be better, and improve our work over time. But no one comes out of the gate being a perfect writer, not even Stephen King, who has sold millions of books all over the world. In his book On Writing, he talks about his awful first drafts, his disgust with his own early writing (he threw it out, only to have it rescued by his wife), and his formula for making stories work (Corrected Draft = First Draft – 10%).

With that being said, no one should be deterred by "not being a writer." The exercises in this book have been designed to facilitate use of the senses, which we all share, and do not require someone to write even one word. Instead, you can choose to record your emotions and stories into a tape recorder.

Other People Tell Stories Better Than We Do

Many of us believe that we are not natural-born storytellers, and that somehow, we inherited all of the interest in stories, but none of the innate ability to construct them. Nonsense. If you have bothered to read this far, and take your time to do the meditations and exercises, I can guarantee that you have a germ of storytelling ability in you. Noticing that stories are important, and agreeing that waking up to the way you use stories in your everyday life is really half the battle. Some of the best writers have become better by incorporating incidents from their own lives into their masterpieces. William Faulkner's Yoknapatawpha County is nothing more or less than the sum of his experiences growing up in the South, with its the dissolution of traditional values and integration of blacks and whites.

72

No one can tell our stories better than we can. The Buddha's last words were reportedly, "Be a lamp unto yourselves," meaning we must move forward knowing that only we can know what it feels like to be us. Only we can tread the path of personal growth and development while having our own unique experiences. And only we can choose to share those experiences with others or to stay silent.

Shyness

This naturally causes some people to feel shy about speaking up. After all, many of us have been brought up to believe that "children should be seen and not heard." Being shy is completely understandable, given today's cultural climate. We are taught to be aggressive, that if we don't reach out and grab something, someone else will. This is hardly a warm and inviting arena in which to bring forth our most intimate stories.

Deciding to share your stories with other people may be a stretch for some, and that's fine. There is no "right" way to conclude your search. Instead, you are the expert. You decide what feels best for you at any particular time in your life. If you are going through a tough divorce, writing down your stories may feel very good for a time. Releasing the anger and confusion may be healing. But it may be too soon to speak the stories out loud. The pain may still be too close and raw, too new.

Being a lamp unto yourself involves getting deeply in touch with what's really happening inside you. This means not letting others push you away from your thoughts, feelings and opinions. It means listening to yourself, more than trying to "talk over" what your mind and body are trying to tell you. Mostly, being a lamp unto yourself means trusting yourself. Chances are, our thoughts and actions are coming from an authentic, considerate place. Learning to trust ourselves is one step towards overcoming the shyness that prevents our true voices from singing out.

We Don't Have the Right to Tell Our Stories

For some reason, many of us believe that a story is only interesting if someone else is telling it. We may feel that our stories are way too personal or revealing about us, and hesitate to share them, believing that we can't possibly expect other people to keep our secrets. Other times, we may feel that only people who have suffered deeply are worthy of our attention, as if suffering just a little is not quite good enough.

I've heard other writers talking about deferring to writers of other genders, races, religions, or economic levels, in a kind of reverse discrimination policy. It may be the cultural norm to reward the victim at this time in our history, but this policy has little relevance to the history of storytelling.

For our purposes, every single being on the planet, and possibly beyond, has the right to tell his or her stories. Since we are not trying to impress other people first and foremost, our duty is not first and foremost to them. We can hold our stories close to us if we choose, or spread them over a wider area by sharing them with others. We tell our stories for many reasons—to heal, to connect, to honor. But we tell them. I believe it's our duty.

If you are a rich person whose only struggle has been how to spend your money, there are stories in you. If you are a refugee from another country, the same is true. If you believe your past spent in boring, middle class suburbia prevents you from telling stories, let me remind you that many of our most successful authors have found much success in suburbia, Sherwood Anderson and Thornton Wilder among them.

We Might Hurt Someone

This is a big one for most people. Since many of us find

74

our first inspiration in whatever has hurt us, we may be afraid of telling the stories as we believe they happened to us. Maybe our mom will find out that we paid someone to take our college finals, or maybe our sister will find out we slept with her boyfriend. Maybe our grandfather will find out once and for all that we believe his breath to be ghastly. Or it could be worse. We could offend a dead ancestor, and risk being haunted.

All of that may be true, but let's take a step back.

At this point, we are engaged in the process of waking up to our stories, that is, to recognize the value of stories in our lives, and to energize ourselves to begin the process of telling them ourselves. Nowhere have we set any ground rules that require you to hurt anyone, or yourself.

Instead, you may choose to "tell" your stories to your notebook, or into your tape recorder. As long as we take care to store these carefully, it's not likely that anyone else will discover what we've said. At this stage, privacy may be the best bet anyway, until you are truly committed to telling your stories out loud.

And don't forget that even if we do decide to use these stories or fragments in the future, we can always change the person's name or blur the physical description enough that there's no way the person would ever be able to recognize him– or herself.

Maybe It Didn't Happen as I Remember It

This is another loaded issue that some of my students have found. At the time I was writing this book, three scandals broke out in the publishing world, all within a few months of one another.

In the first, memoirist James Frey was revealed by the

Smoking Gun as having fabricated parts of his memoir *A Million Little Pieces,* which had been chosen by Oprah Winfrey for her Book Club. The second was when author JT Leroy was revealed to have been a non-existent person, a hoax made up by two people. Lastly, author Nasdijj (revealed to be a Michigan man who is white) posed as a Navajo Indian to get his book *The Blood Runs Like a River Through My Dreams* published by Ballantine. In the cases of Frey and Nasdijj, books were recalled and destroyed, or relabeled as fiction. Frey also lost a book deal with Riverhead, as well as several film and television deals, in light of the scandal.

With all that being said, it is of course crucial to tell the truth. The entire process of waking up to our stories depends on a hard look at our lives, and the dedication to living authentic lives in the future. In writing down the rough draft of your story, however, it may be fine simply to record what your memory calls forth. For now, try not to judge what comes up. It's all important information, assisting you to delve deeper and deeper into the mystery of your self.

In Chapter 10, we will talk about the role of memory, and how to make sure we're not fooling ourselves with our storytelling. For now, let's concentrate on allowing memories and story fragments to come forward. In time, we'll decide how to shape them into longer works.

It's Only Good if I'm Going to Publish It

Many of you may be interested in publishing your stories, or possibly using them as the basis for longer works, such as novels, novellas, or screenplays. That is wonderful and very ambitious work. For many, writing and telling stories is a very lonely pursuit. We work alone all day long, seldom coming into contact with others except at workshops, readings, and conferences. Publishing is a way of attaining the closure that sometimes does not come naturally in the act of writing.

However, if we all waited until someone wanted to publish our stories, we'd be waiting a very long time, and very few stories would be told. Most literary magazines, where short stories are frequently published, have tiny operating budgets, and must be extremely cutthroat about which stories they select for publication.

Waiting for others to choose us may also feel very demoralizing and personalized. That's why I really like the notion of self-publishing, in 'zines, grassroots literary magazines, and on the Web. Waiting for others to approve of us may be the way it appears that success is attained. But this may be another way we allow gatekeepers to retain the power that is rightly ours.

Your work is valid, whether you cannot spell, form sentences, or even think straight. That's what this book is for. It's designed to help you find your way to the very thought processes that give rise to the greatest emotional expression. No author started out as a genius. At some point, all of your favorites were exactly where you are now. Giving yourself a break to just create, without hearing those little voices of dismay and judgement over your shoulder, is the only way to be truly alive.

In this chapter, I have laid out the most popular ways we tend to stand in the way of telling our stories. Remember that our silence is a form of complicity that allies us with whatever we feel is wrong with our lives. By not doing something about the very things we complain about, we form a union with them. And the only way out is to assume the power that telling our stories confers upon us.

Meditation:

This week, we're going to use our meditation sessions in a slightly different way. After the Base Practice, I want you to start to detect where you stand in your own way of telling your stories. We will begin the process of opening up to the critical voices in our heads that may have shut us down in the past.

Once we have identified what these voices are saying, we'll work a bit on adopting strategies to release them or keep them at bay.

Try to notice, as the days pass, if your voices sound like anyone you know. Do they speak with a certain cadence, like your uncle? Do they have a slight accent, like your first grade teacher? Each little detail is one more tool in your arsenal to help fight these damning voices.

- Go into your meditation space and close the door. By now, this should have become habitual. Perhaps you do your meditation exercises at a certain part of the day, or delineate it with other activities, such as between work and dinner, or between the gym and work. As always, make sure no one will disturb you for at least twenty minutes.

- Find your way into your meditation posture. This, too, should be rote by now. Try not to have to look in the mirror to get yourself upright but relaxed. Instead, try to feel your way into the pose, using whatever means you have to make yourself comfortable. Remember not to force yourself into the position, or strain your muscles trying to hold yourself stiffly.

- Close your eyes. Allow your breath to come at its normal pace. Even if you are breathing hard from stress or exercise, allow that to just be. Notice the thoughts that are moving through your mind. By now, they may seem sort of funny to you, or like familiar company. I like to acknowledge my thoughts like old friends.

- Now imagine that your thoughts are liquid, and there is a hole at the center of your forehead. Imagine your thoughts dripping out of the hole, cascading down your face, onto your clothing, and then the floor. Your thoughts are not

Wake Up to Your Stories

dirty or stagnant, but akin to cleansing water. Feel how refreshing it is to have your thoughts leave you in this way.

- By now, you may feel that your mind is empty, or that only one or two thoughts remain behind. That's fine. Begin your Basic Practice, labeling your thoughts as they arise and following your breath in and out. Notice the tenor of your thoughts now. Are they entirely practical thoughts? More fantasy-oriented? How are they the same or different from your normal thoughts?

- Connect with each of your senses from the bottom of your body to the top. First connect with your sense of touch, using your fingers to sense the world that surrounds you right now. Label that "touching" in your mind. Likewise, move up to the mouth, the nose, the ears and finally the eyes, labeling each sense to yourself. Notice if this is easier or harder than it has been in past weeks. If it is harder this time, what is standing in the way? Are there worries encompassing your time for yourself? Just notice them and let them reside in your mind, without trying to chase them away.

- Along with the worries that may be distracting you from your Base Practice, try to notice the emotions that are running through you right now. Again, the goal is not to chase away emotions or somehow dull them. They are an authentic part of your experience, and will help to identify the stories that are important to your life. Rather than trying to "solve" the issues behind your prevailing emotions, just touch them lightly with your consciousness, as if to say, "I see you."

- Now check in with your body. Are there any areas that may need to be readjusted? Any specific tightness that seems new or different from other times you've meditated?

- Now we're going to try something new. Without lying

down completely, or making your body prone, try to relax as much as you can. Take your time, if you need to allow your breathing to slow. When you are ready, take five breaths, saying "thinking" each time you notice a thought coming into your mind. By now, you may begin to notice that you can label a thought before it really blooms into a fully flowering storyline in your mind.

- Now invite the critical little voices to step forward in your mind. I call these the Little Destroyers, because they seem so intent on letting us go a little way towards our goals and dreams, then taking great pleasure in smashing them. I'm sure it wouldn't be as fun for them if we hadn't started out towards a goal in the first place, and gotten a head start with our expectations. It wouldn't be nearly as rewarding for the Little Destroyers, the little wreckers of dreams.

- What are your Little Destroyers saying to you? If you feel comfortable, let them spill out everything they want to say. Remember, it's only in your mind, and has no ability to hurt you in the present moment. Are your Little Destroyers angry with you for not spending more time on meeting other people's needs? For being selfish and high falutin? For trying to step outside the boundaries society may have drawn for you? Listen carefully to the Little Destroyers. They are our teachers, and we can learn a lot from them.

- Also notice what changes take place in you as you open yourself up and listen carefully to the Little Destroyers, without judging them or closing down to what they have to say. Have your emotions changed, and if so, how? If your current emotion had a color, what would it be? What changes do you notice in your body? Have you begun to hold yourself a certain way, or feel unbalanced somehow? As with the other exercises, just take a few moments to notice and validate what you feel in your

Wake Up to Your Stories

mind and body. No need to change anything now. This is where you are, and it is important.

- When your Little Destroyers have completely exhausted themselves, spilling out every possible reason for why you should not be engaging in this practice, thank them and allow them to ride your "out" breath when you exhale. Expel all of that angry, frustrated, suffering energy with your breath. It may even feel good to let the breath out with a little snap of the abdomen, making sure every last bit of it has left your lungs.

- Return to your regular breathing, taking slow, deep inhalations and filling your lungs with fresh new air. Feel yourself as a vessel to be filled, with oxygen, with food, water, sleep and other nurturing things. Take five full breaths here, letting the voices of your Little Destroyers, as well as the feelings that may have come up for you, to dissolve. Then go back to your regular meditation for one minute, allowing your mind to clear.

Exercise:

When you come out of your meditation, please immediately record your observations, using your notebook or cassette recorder. As closely as you can, capture what the Little Destroyers said to you. If you can, recall their tone of voice, little affectations in speech, or even accents. Many permutations have come up for students of mine. Some have not recognized who this person (or combination of people) is until much later. It may even be a character your mind has made up to store this information for you.

If you can record the Little Destroyers' words, so much the better. Writing it out like a dialogue can be helpful. If not, though, that's fine, too. The most important aspect of this exercise is to point out why you may believe you aren't supposed to tell your stories.

When you are finished writing down as much as you can remember about what the Little Destroyers said, write down how you felt at the beginning of the meditation. How did that change as you moved through the meditation exercise, and how do you feel now, as you record what occurred? Remember to date the entry with your pen or your voice, so you will be able to refer back to it later.

Now let's compare what your Little Destroyers were saying to the list of six main ways we tend to use our stories in our everyday lives:

- Healing from Abuse or Neglect
- Connecting with Relatives and Family Members
- To Leave Something Behind
- To Express Ourselves and the World We Live In
- To Become More Visible
- To Ensure That Our Way of Life Continues

Refer back to the one that appealed to you most last week. Does that still ring true now, or has it shifted? Either choice is fine, as long as it's authentic for you at this moment of your life.

Now let's look at what your Little Destroyers said to you. Were its words consistent with the choice you made? For instance, if you chose "to become more visible," and your Little Destroyers read you the riot act about "making a big deal of yourself," or "wanting to be better than everyone else," or "needing to be different from other people," you have established a very important connection. Your Little Destroyers are actually helping you figure out why you want to tell stories, and perhaps what types of stories will yield the richest results for you.

Spend a few minutes recording your observations about the connection between the ways you want to or currently do use your stories, and what your Little Destroyers have revealed to you. Most people report feeling very empowered when they discover this connection. There is no right emotion, though, and if you feel sadness creeping up, or another painful feeling, please give yourself a few minutes to record these feelings and then let them go.

During this week and next, you may wish to give yourself a bit more time for your meditation sessions, perhaps thirty minutes or so, so you are able to recover, should any troubling emotions come up for you.

As always, please record any seemingly random thoughts, memory fragments or storylines you remember, from today or another time in your life. We are now one third of the way through the process of waking up to your stories, and hopefully, you have already begun to notice a change in yourself.

Follow-Up:

As you move through the activities of your week, please remember to carve some time out for yourself and your Base Practice. At some point during each day, connect each of your senses to your mind, until it's almost impossible to disconnect your senses from your feelings and the thoughts that move through your mind.

While you're doing the Base Practice, notice when the Little Destroyers try to butt in and have their way with your mind. Are your thoughts easily swayed to "their" way of thinking? Are the two ways of being so closely entwined that it's impossible to separate them? Have you adopted certain ways of coping with them, and if so, how?

On each day of the week, dedicate your attention to the Little Destroyers. On at least one occasion per day, try to notice the sly ways they might attempt to sidle into your consciousness. Did they undermine your confidence before a meeting with a big client? Cause you to say something you didn't mean to a friend? Stop you from trying something new?

Record the words of the Little Destroyers, as well as the effect these words had on you, both internally and externally. Rather than forming any concretized judgements about yourself or the possible source behind the Little Destroyers, just see them for what they are: attempts made by your unconscious mind to sabotage what you want to do. The Little Destroyers stand in the way of our waking up to our stories, and they stand in the way of us making real progress in our lives. Just starting to notice these attempts at sabotage will really begin to open your mind.

If you find yourself in a very challenging position, and the Little Destroyers are doing a real number on you, step back a bit, mentally and emotionally. If you need to, resort to your Base Practice, breathing slowly and steadily and labeling your thoughts as "thinking." Within a few minutes, you may notice that the "heat" behind the stressful emotions has lessened.

Keep a record of all the emotions behind these episodes. Begin to see connections between the external challenges you may face in the world and the appearances of the Little Destroyers in your mind. These connections are different for each person, so if you are doing these exercises with a friend, don't be surprised if you have wildly different experiences.

Do any symbols come up time and again? For example, do the Little Destroyers come forward when you're dealing with an authority figure, such as a boss or your father? Do they speak loudest when you have to deal with a stranger? A lover or intimate friend? With yourself?

Next week, we'll begin the process of taming our fears, and adopting strategies to keep the Little Destroyers at bay, or release them altogether. The strands of information you're gathering about yourself may seem disconnected now. But these strands can be woven together into a very accurate and moving picture of who you are today, and who you can become in the future.

5 Taming Our Fears

"As I look at the human story I see two stories. They run parallel and never meet. One is of people who live, as they can or must, the events that arrive; the other is of people who live, as they intend, the events they create."

— Margaret Anderson

I t's been four weeks now that you've been engaging in this process of waking up to your stories, and I would like to congratulate you for having the tenacity to look so deeply into yourself. The path of self-development receives a lot of press, and can be paid a good deal of lip service. But to really tread this path requires a great deal of courage. If you have come this far, you have proven that you are a person who has the stamina to make it all the way through this program.

What sorts of changes have you noticed in yourself since last week? Have you noticed shifts in your needs or personal goals? And how has this affected your desire to nurture yourself in an ongoing way?

So far, we have seen that each of takes part in stories as

they relate to us externally, in groups or with our families. We have also seen that they take place internally, as storylines we create for our relationships with others, and ourselves.

This week, we'll focus our meditation and exercises on taming the fears that may have come up last week. The Little Destroyers are often the most vocal of our fears, but sometimes there are additional layers underneath these, still to be discovered. As we discover those additional layers, we can begin to release them, or find ways to keep them from derailing our plans and desires.

Let's take a minute to check in from last week:

- Did you do your meditation exercises every day?

- How did your Little Destroyers appear in your meditation sessions?

- Did they speak with a particular cadence or accent? Or choose unique words?

- What emotions came up for you during these meditation sessions?

- Which way of using stories did you gravitate towards originally, and how was this changed by noticing the Little Destroyers?

- Were you able to notice the Little Destroyers in your day-to-day life?

- In what type of situations did the Little Destroyers tend to appear?

- Which emotions came up for you at these times?

- What kinds of emotional connections were you able to make from the exercises of this past week?

- Finally, how are you feeling about yourself as a result of these practices?

As always, take a minute to look into yourself before starting this chapter. Do a quick glance through your body and your emotions. Are you feeling any pain or tension anywhere? Are there any overly upsetting emotions? If so, note them down in your notebook or speak them into your recorder. Accept that this is where you are today, and it is completely fine for now.

Receiving Our Stories

As far as stories are concerned, most of us are used to being on the receiving end of things. We are familiar with having stories told to us as children, and move into our lives hearing stories from others. Sometimes, these stories are told about us, such as an anecdote at a family party. Other times, they are told to us in more culturally established ways, such as on television, or in books and movies. Because we experience the stories from this second category en masse, we form opinions that are, by definition, impersonal. Instead, we become influenced by what others are thinking or talking about. What may have been designed to be a unique and powerful statement for an individual, the art or creation itself, has now been transformed into a trend or a movement.

Because we are generally in the process of receiving stories, it has become very easy for us to be influenced by the tools of the media. We internalize ideas about how our bodies should look, how we should behave and even who we should love because of ideas launched from these platforms.

Of course, the tools of the media are not all bad. All of us are likely to remember at least one song, movie, book or television show that moved us or made us think about our own circumstances in a more mindful way. But subsuming our collective need to share our stories in some way contributes to these dark trends. The makers of toothpaste may want to sell us white teeth on television. But the only way to counteract these messages is to tell stories of our own, especially those that drive home the message that there is no such thing as a truly "white" tooth. A thousand diet books may have been launched on the fears we all have of not being attractive or desirable enough. Again, the best weapon to fight these messages is to tell stories about proud grandmothers, and the fact that their achievements have exactly matched their size.

Our stories are not just integral to the way we live, they are crucial to our development as a culture. Without them, we lose our uniqueness, and become part of a boring, homogenized mass, devoid of life or soul. By always being on the receiving end of our stories, we allow others to create history, as if we never existed. Correspondingly, we do not have an impact on our culture.

What does your experience look like? What does it feel like to be you?

What smells and sounds permeate your days? Which tastes bring back the most potent memories?

What does touching your very first toy remind you of? What feelings does it unleash in you?

If we let others do the storytelling, we've signed off on allowing them to tell us what the world looks like, what it smells and sounds and tastes like. What our favorite toys were, and how it felt to play with them. Because of this, it becomes our duty to search out our personal stories and share them with others. We make our lives richer as a result of this, and narrow the gap of difference between us.

Fear, and the Fear of Fear Itself

The word fear has come to have a negative connotation for us. As children, we're told to "suck it up," and continue moving towards whatever scares us. Boys especially are called names if they don't want to participate in contact sports or playground fights, but girls are not immune from this, either.

Each of us came into the world programmed with various fears to ensure our survival. On some level we know, once we've reached our hands into a fire and come out burned, not to touch it again. Our psychological circuitry acts quicker than we can even form a thought about it. Because of this, we are able to store knowledge that is useful to us at other times.

So fear can have a very healthy use. After all, it's best that we don't try walking into traffic without looking, flying a plane without taking some lessons, or trying to tame a wild bull with no exit strategy. Every day, we use our stored fears as a way of retaining stability and equanimity.

However, as we have begun to see, fear can also arise in ways that are counterproductive. Because fears can be stored as a result of physical instances, in the tissues of the body or, as a result of emotional instances, in the brain, they can be tricky to root out. Their terrific speed, faster than the mind can process them, also makes them tough to track. Are we really having that feeling, we may ask ourselves, or is that just a passing hiccup in our emotional system?

In the metaphysical community, fear has been labeled a negative or malevolent force, which is intent on keeping us from our most precious dreams. But to settle for this is to overlook some of the wonderful uses of fear. Fear keeps us from going back to a lover who has mistreated us. Fear keeps us from staying with an abusive parent. Fear can be the galvanizing emotion that gets us out of a bad job, a boring town, or a stultifying school.

"Let me assert my firm belief that the only thing we have to fear is fear itself—nameless, unreasoning, unjustified terror which paralyzes needed efforts to convert retreat into advance," said President Franklin Delano Roosevelt, at his first inaugural address.

In waking up to our stories, it's important to strike a balance with our fears. On one hand, we can respect that fear keeps us from harm. On the other, we can work with our fears to make sure they do not block us from truly experiencing life with all of our senses, or paralyzing our efforts to convert retreat into advance.

Boundaries

One of the most important uses of fear is to help us establish healthy boundaries. Sometimes, we may meet someone new and want to spend every minute with him or her. We may dream about this person when we're not together, or even fantasize about the kind of future we might enjoy together. But all it takes is one little moment to put doubt in your mind. Did he forget to call me back, or is he mad at me? Did she mean to call me that other person's name, or does that really mean she's tired of me?

In this example, fear is the emotion that comes in, immediately following on the heels of doubt. Wait, it says. Put on the brakes! At times like these, fear is trying to warn you that moving too fast in a certain direction may not be healthy. Maybe the other person's action didn't mean anything at all, but your emotions have come in to warn you that, without even realizing it, you may have been writing a story that's potentially dangerous for you.

What is fear asking you to wait for?

In learning to tame our fears, it's good to look at what those fears may be, or even what they're tied to in our minds. As we've found so far, our minds are usually not perfectly linear and organized. Our synapses fire, and we don't really know where that electrical current is going to take us. That's why electrical circuits exist in a closed system, and why they have to have circuit breakers built in for safety. In our case, fear acts as a circuit breaker, providing the protection we may be lacking when external circumstances may not correspond with what our emotions want to happen.

Fearing Our Own Nature

As we begin to notice the ways we experience and express fear, it's important to also combine this search with what we have found out about ourselves so far. We have discovered ways we keep silent about our feelings and our stories. We have talked about our need for stories, and the way we tend to use them in our day-to-day reality. Finally, we have begun to unearth what stands in the way of us sharing our stories.

Looking at your notebooks, or listening to the recordings you've made over the past few weeks, you may begin to notice an obvious pattern. All of our trepidation may exist because of the same person. All of our bad memories may tend to feature the same scenario. The reason we need stories in the first place is to heal from what a certain person did to us.

But for many, the connections may be subtler than that. Our fear may not be concentrated around a certain person or place, it may not even have a destination or source. It is simply fear of what might come up when we begin searching inside ourselves. Some may fear that their lives will become uncontrollable, or that they will not be able to go on with things as they had been doing. Others may just not trust their own emotional systems, or view people who show too much emotion as weak, needy, or pathetic.

If this is true of you, accept it. There is no shame in being this way, nor is there any real benefit. It just is. And because this is so, it may be best to watch your emotions as we move through this week's meditation and follow-up exercises. The "heat" behind your emotions, as well as the emotions themselves, are important when it comes to unraveling the stories inside you.

In time, you may find that you are able to move further into your fears, with less of an emotional reaction. But for now, moving close enough to begin working with the fears is good enough. Fear of our own inner nature is not a new thing, but it is potentially an obstacle, which keeps us from attaining all we wish.

Welcoming Fear

It may seem like a strange idea to welcome fear, but some people do it all the time. We are a culture of extreme sports enthusiasts, of people who hurl themselves off bridges tied only by a string around their waists, or drive at reckless speeds on muddy tracks, seemingly oblivious to the potential of danger. Some of us flock to "amusement" parks, where we fly through the air on terrifying roller coasters or are dropped from several stories high to plummet to the ground.

The people who partake in these activities may understand a certain kind of fear, and want to tame it by facing the physical sensations that come with the territory. They may become addicted to the increased heart rate and blood flow that comes from the physiological changes to the body when they attempt these things.

Similarly, when we confront what we found out about ourselves last week, the very things that stand in the way of our telling our stories, we may experience physiological changes such as increased breathing and heart rate, sharpened awareness, sweating, and a dry mouth. Perhaps not so coincidentally, we tell stories with our mouths. That connection is an interesting one to consider.

In yoga and Ayurvedic (Indian) medicine, there are seven chakras, or energy centers, that run through the body. They range from the root chakra, found in the genitals, to the crown chakra, at the very top of the head, and are placed all along the spinal column. The fifth of these is the throat chakra, which governs communication, growth and expression. It is associated with the color blue, and this area tends to experience pressure or pain when we are not expressing our emotions properly.

Fear, as we have seen, constricts this area of our body, among others, preparing us for battle or escape. So when we start to write down our feelings and stories, or God forbid, tell them to someone else, we may find that our throats dry up or become scratchy. We may cough or ask for water. We may feel like we're getting a cold. These are all signs that there is something underneath our desire to express ourselves. And that "something" is usually fear.

Fear is an excellent escape artist, cloaking itself in all kinds of pretty clothing. It can make it seem like we're doing ourselves a favor ("If you take out the garbage every day, we can talk about this storytelling thing you want to do."), as if we're protecting ourselves ("Wouldn't all that writing and meditating only make you more tired than you already are?"), or as if we're being nurturing to ourselves ("Why don't we spend some money on some new shoes instead of telling stories?"). But underneath all of these behaviors is the fear of getting closer to ourselves, and really, the fear of the fear itself. We may be terrified that we have a fear. Terrified to admit it, to act on it, to share it with other people.

That's the reason I like to welcome my fear, at least when I can recognize it as fear. I imagine my fear as a watchdog, sitting at the door of my life. I see it guarding the door for predators, not allowing anything dangerous to come any closer. I feed my fear nutritious food and fresh water two times daily. I pet its furry head and go back to my writing.

Other times, I see my fear as an overly concerned friend. I'm pretty sure we all know a few of those or, if not, a few overly concerned family members. My fear loves tea, and when I make it a steaming cup of Lemon Zinger, it sits at my table and doesn't even notice that I am doing things that would ordinarily horrify it. I meditate and look mindfully into myself. I write about what I have seen, about the way I am.

94   *Wake Up to Your Stories*

There is an old saying: "Keep your friends close, but your enemies closer," attributed to everyone from The Godfather's Michael Corleone to Julius Caesar. In the same way, you may find that keeping your fear close is the best defense. Inviting it into your life, rather than trying to push it away, may even give you a warm feeling towards it. After all, your fear is only trying to protect you, just like your parents once protected you from exploring that intriguingly tall tree, when at the time you felt you were big enough to climb it. You may not be partial to tea, but you can invite your fear into your life in other ways, as you would with a friend. Maybe you can watch a movie together, have lunch, or go shopping. The best activities involve something slightly mundane, so that in time, your fear of writing and sharing your stories is about as scary as brushing your teeth in the morning.

Know that your fear is not necessarily your enemy. Dedicate yourself to getting to know it, including the warning signs that are unique to your personality. Do you get giddy and silly? Distracted? Dark and somber?

Tell your fear that you appreciate the work it does for you, but that you also need the freedom to explore yourself. Fear, if left unchecked, can produce many of the same long term effects as stress, including chronic pain, elevated blood pressure, fatigue, sleeplessness, and immune disorders. Even your fear doesn't want you to experience these things. It wants, despite the results it may cause, to keep you from harm.

Meditation:

This week's meditation exercise will focus on the fears that may come up as we wake up to our stories. Once we begin to recognize these inner voices, physiological changes and resulting behaviors as fears, we will adopt strategies to tame them.

This week, I would like you to attune yourself very carefully to the tiniest changes in you. Remember that fear may look like something else completely, another emotion, or a certain repetitive behavior. Only you will know if what you are experiencing is covering over your fear, or is simply an authentic emotion, asking to be acted upon.

Even though this may sound like a daunting week, or a daunting exercise, please don't forget to have fun with it. Sharing stories should be occasions to revel in our common humanity, whether sad, silly or saucy. If you find yourself thinking inappropriate thoughts, this may be another way you cloak your fear. Watch out!

- Find your way to your private meditation spot and close the door. Give yourself at least thirty to forty-five minutes to do the meditation exercise and follow-up writing to process your experiences and feelings.

- Adopt your meditation posture, with your legs crossed in front of you, or flat on the floor, if you are seated in a chair. Again, please do not lie down unless it's absolutely necessary. This is only likely to dilute your focus and overly relax you, so that you won't be able to see your fears as they arise.

- As you settle into your meditation posture, relax your individual body parts. Feel your body as it sits in a position of complete balance. Notice all parts of your body by feeling the way they fit together and support you in your meditation posture.

- Now watch your breath as it moves through your mouth, into your throat and down into your lungs and belly. Fill your body completely with air and let it out slowly. If it takes a few minutes to breathe calmly, so be it. Allow yourself that time. Begin your Base Practice, acknowledging your thoughts by labeling them and letting them leave you with the out breath.

96

- Notice the type of thoughts you're having now, if you're having any at all. Are you worried about the future? Stressed about the past? Nervous about the present? Allow whatever emotions are there for you to come forward, without judgement. Take five full breaths here.

- Now connect each one of your senses to the meditation, moving from the bottom of your body upward. Feel your fingers as they take in data from the surrounding atmosphere, including temperature, and label that "touching." Feel your mouth, lips and tongue as they register the world, and label that "tasting." Feel your nose as it filters your breath and label that "smelling." Feel your ears as they sense any sound in the room and label that "hearing." Finally, feel your eyes, whether open or closed, as they take in visual information, and label that "seeing." Take five more full breaths here.

- Notice the emotions you're having now. Are they neutral, or weighted in a particular direction? Is there a lot of "heat" behind the emotion? Has it shifted from when you began this meditation session? Let these feelings rest in you for a few breaths, letting them know that you will not kick them out.

- Now we're going to begin the process of welcoming our fears. Repeat the word fear in your mind, allowing it to roll around a little bit. What comes to mind? Do you see an image in your mind? Have a feeling in your body? Now I'd like you to visualize yourself writing (or speaking) your stories, just on your own. What do you see when you see yourself doing this? Is there a particular goal in mind— to be published, for example? Do you feel like you have to hide your stories from other people? As if you are taking valuable time away from something else?

- What kinds of feelings come up for you when you visualize yourself telling your stories, even if it's just in private?

Some may notice that they have already begun to have bodily reactions to this imagery. Are you tensing up in the shoulder area? Do you feel sick to your stomach? Or does the thought of telling your stories not feel like much in your body? Take a minute to notice what your body is doing now.

- Now visualize yourself sharing your stories with others. You may see yourself in a group setting of likeminded storytellers, listening and speaking in turn, or by yourself, reading your stories at a bookstore. Once you have the image you want firmly in your mind, take a minute to notice the feelings you're having now. Are they the same as when you were telling the stories on your own, or have they changed somehow? If so, what's different about them?

- Check in with your body again, to see if the physical feelings you were having a moment ago are the same or different from the ones you may be having now. Do you need to change your meditation posture to better support yourself? If so, take the time to do so now.

- Locate the strongest feeling you have had in the past two exercises and hold it in your mind, along with the corresponding visualization. Now let's look deeper, asking a few question to clarify our experience:

- Are you afraid of hurting someone else?

- Are you afraid of your own truth, and getting to know yourself intimately?

- Are you afraid that your memory can't be trusted, and that things didn't happen the way you remember them?

- Do you believe you don't have the time to tell your stories?

- Do you believe you're not qualified to tell your stories,

98

that you're "not a writer?"

- Do you believe that others are better storytellers than you are?

- Are you overly shy about telling and sharing your stories?

- Do you believe that you don't have the right to tell your stories?

- Are your stories only worth telling if they are going to be published?

- Notice which of these options really stands out for you, the one that really seems to pinpoint your feelings most closely. Now ask yourself: What is the worst thing that could happen if I decided to tell my stories? Let the image unfold in your mind (knowing that this is, in itself, a story). Allow yourself to truly feel all the terrible things you believe might happen to your life.

- In your mind, label this "fear." This is a very popular time for the Little Destroyers to make an appearance, so notice them as well. You have had some practice with these destructive voices now, and have the tools you need to combat them, so don't worry about it for now. Check in with your emotions and your bodily sensations, so you will begin to recognize the internal and external signs of fear in the future.

- Now see this fear as a person or object. I like to see mine as wearing a funny polka-dot floppy hat, so it will seem less threatening. Your fear may be a bubble, a bucket, or a short, old woman with gray hair. Make it as personal as you like, adding details until the image seems very memorable to you.

- In your mind, invite the fear inside your home, to your table. Ask your fear if it would like something to eat or drink. No matter how demanding the fear is, no matter what exotic delicacy it may want, it's there in your refrigerator or in your kitchen cabinets. Prepare something for your fear and bring it to the table.

- Offer the drink, snack or meal to your fear as you would a friend, making sure it has a napkin for its lap and honey for its tea. If you want to, talk to your fear in your mind, trying to make it feel welcome.

- When you have exchanged pleasantries with your fears, explain to it that you want to try something new in your life. You believe that waking up to your stories will help with your development, and that you will be able to meet certain personal goals with its help, such as nurturing your relationships, healing your past, or asking for what you're worth. You would appreciate its help in meeting these needs, because you understand that your fear works very hard to ensure your protection. Thank your fear for spending much, if not all, of its time making sure you're unharmed. Communicate that it will always have a friendly place at your table, and that it is welcome to drop by at any time.

- How does your fear react to your explanation? Does it seem reasonable or hard-headed? Is it able to communicate feelings, or just issue orders? Does it talk back to you and, if so, what does it say?

- Now shift your attention to your body, registering any changes that may have occurred there. Do you feel tenser or more relaxed? Is there a specific area of your body that you're noticing more than others, and if so, why?

- Return to your Base Practice, breathing deeply and allowing your thoughts to be labeled as they leave you on the out breath. Fill your·lungs with air five times, letting go of your fear, and all of the feelings you may have experienced, as you release the air from your body. As your mind clears, come out of the meditation.

Exercise:

Allow yourself to resituate yourself when you come out of the meditation. Give yourself a few moments of time to come back to reality. When you feel ready, record the experiences you had in the meditation. How did your fear appear to you? Were you able to dress it in certain clothes, or control it in any way? How did your fear act when you invited it in? Was it surprised? Anxious? Angry? Compliant?

Did your fear say anything to you and, if so, what did it say?

As with last week's meditation, try to write out the conversation between you and your fear. If you heard a particular way of speaking, an accent or affectation, write it down. If you had an argument, write that down. Just let it all spill out of you in a rush of words. Bypass that Little Destroyer that wants to dam up your words before they leave your mind.

What reasons did your fear give for not wanting you to tell your stories? Was it one of the following?:

- Maybe my memory is off, and doesn't recall things as they really happened.

- I have no time for storytelling.

- I'm not qualified to tell my stories.

- Others are much better storytellers than I am.

- I'm too shy.

- I don't have the right to tell my stories.

• Why bother, if my stories aren't going to be published?

If so, how did your fear go about trying to convince you to give up telling your stories? Was it sly in assuring you that it's not good for you? Did it manage to tame any worries you might have, by saying to forget that silly old storytelling?

Now record what changes your body went through as it moved through the various parts of the meditation. Did you move from relaxation to stiffness, or the other way around? Did your fear seem to lodge in any particular part of your body? When you invited it in for tea, did that change anything in what your body was feeling?

Lastly, record how this meditation measured up with you expectations. Did you expect to tame your fears with a chair and whip? How was your experience the same or different from this mental image? If you had another expectation altogether, write that down. If you had none, that's fine, too.

Can you see that inviting your fear into your life, and nurturing it like anything else that looks out for you is, in a sense, taming it? Connect with the feeling that what you perceive to be harmful does not have to be met with force in order to "conquer" it. Allow that feeling to permeate your entire being. Feel the sense of power that comes from not having to fight all the time.

How do you feel now? Record your internal and external reactions to the meditation session, and your post-meditation processing.

This is the longest meditation session we'll do in this program of waking up to our stories. During this week, try to find a bit more time for yourself. You may find that your fears change from day to day, or from week to week. You may find that your fear is very reasonable on one day, and irascible the next. If so, try not to schedule anything important right after your meditation sessions. I find that it's best to ease out of these sessions by doing something necessary but ultimately rewarding, such as talking with a trusted friend, reading a great book, or making a nutritious meal. You may not feel like talking to anyone afterwards, or not anyone who requires you to be anyone other than who you are right now.

If you have any additional thoughts, please record them now. Many of my students have said that this exercise often releases memories. If so, don't judge your memories or try to filter them. For those who have already been writing before this program, don't try to "write" your memories, by prettying the words and sentence structure. Simply let them come out however they want. There is plenty of time later for structure and editing.

Congratulations! You now have one very powerful tool to help you deal with your fears as they come up in your stories, and in other parts of your life.

Follow-Up:

Since this week's meditation is longer and somewhat more complicated than in previous weeks, we'll keep the follow-up short and sweet.

This week is a crucial one in your development as a storyteller. You stand on the precipice, between thinking about telling your stories and actually doing it. More than ever, you may be tempted to blow off your meditation sessions for any number of reasons. You may say you're too tired, too burdened, too untalented, or too emotionally drained. What you are is scared, but that's fine. So is everybody else.

Please do your Base Practice every day this week, taking a minute at the beginning of each session to connect to your senses. Then, as you engage your fear, try to notice changes in yourself, both internally and externally.

Over the course of the week, see if you can draw a little closer to your fear. See if you can invite it in a little more, or become a fraction of an inch less afraid of it. If it will have a conversation with you, try to reasonably explain your wishes to tell your stories. If your fear keeps harping on a particular way in which you might screw up your life, not to mention the lives of those close to you, remain steady in your arguments. Know that you do not have to resort to yelling or anger to get your way with your fear. Ultimately, you govern it. It doesn't govern you.

Try bringing this practice into your daily life. On each day this week, try to notice your fears as they arise. Do they come up at the same time every day? Around the same person? When you are asked to do a particular thing? Becoming intimate with your fears' patterns is another way of drawing closer to them, and ultimately making friends.

Did your fears stop you from doing anything this week? Did you let them talk you out of trying something new? Or did you find your fears relaxing somewhat, and admitting that maybe you have a point about wanting to share your stories with others?

If your fears become overwhelming this week, back off temporarily. If need be, go back to your Base Practice, labeling your fears as thoughts when then come up, and allowing them to leave your mind when you breathe out.

Next week, we'll use this technique of taming our fears as we begin to locate the common threads in our lives. By holding our fears close, we are waking up to the stories that have been living inside us all along, and opening ourselves to love.

6 Awakening Love

"*Self-love, my liege, is not so vile a sin as self-neglecting.*"

— William Shakespeare, King Henry V. Act ii. Sc. 4.

Five weeks have passed, and we're moving steadily towards a better working knowledge of ourselves, and the stories we may be drawn to telling. We have identified our needs, our personal stumbling blocks, and the fears that keep them firmly in place. Now it's time to connect with what we love most about the world, the act of telling stories and ultimately, ourselves.

But before we begin with that, let's check in to see how you did last week:

- Did you get to do your meditation exercises every day?

- Were you able to engage with your fears?

- Did your fears have readily identifiable characteristics, such as an accent or unique clothing?

- What did you find yourself feeling as you engaged with your fears?

- Has your way of using stories changed as a result of this exercise?

- Were you able to notice and engage with your fears as they appeared in your day-to-day life?

- If so, did they appear in a particular context, with a particular person, or at a particular time of day?

- Were you able to make any new connections about yourself as a result of this week's exercise?

- Finally, have you noticed any changes in yourself, in your outward attitude towards your life, or even internally, towards yourself?

Now let's deepen your check-in a bit more:

- How have you shifted your perspective since you began the program? If you need some inspiration, look back at your notes from the first week, or listen to the recordings you made at that time. Notice how you have changed, even if it's only a little bit. Notice the parts of you that remain the same.

- Have your goals changed?

- Do you look at storytelling in a new way?

- How have your needs changed, in terms of your storytelling and practical lives? Please take a minute to record the changes you have noticed about yourself, both inside and out.

- Have you noticed yourself getting involved with the storylines of others, or allowing others to tell your stories for you?

- If not, what strategies have you adopted in this part of your life?

When you're finished considering the answers to these

questions, or speaking them into your recorder, take a moment to reflect on what you have accomplished so far. How does your body feel today? Are there any tensions or worries being stored there? And how are you feeling emotionally? Record everything you are. It is just as valuable as yesterday, and tomorrow, and the day after that.

(What's So Funny 'Bout) Peace, Love and Understanding?

Elvis Costello sings one of my favorite songs of all time, taking what was once a relatively mild song recorded by writer Nick Lowe's band Brinsley Schwarz and turning it into one of the most snarling protest songs ever. Leave it to an angry singer to ask the most obvious question: why is peace, love and understanding funny? Has it all become a joke to us? Are we too cool or jaded to recognize the humanity in our fellow human beings? And why do we only notice other people when someone's practically screaming at us? The juxtaposition of these two elements makes Costello's version of this song a classic.

Similarly, now that we've begun to get a handle on our needs, the way we tend to use stories, what stands in our way, and the fears we've associated with storytelling, it's time to turn that on its head, and begin to combine the scary and the off-putting with what we're all striving for anyway.

Peace

Hopefully, you have begun to find a sense of peace in establishing and maintaining a daily meditation practice. People tend to think of peace as a word with only one meaning: devoid of conflict or war. But this week, we'll find that this word has many meanings, all of which are directly applicable to the process of waking up to our stories.

Thich Nhat Hahn is a Vietnamese Buddhist monk

whose country was profoundly affected by the Vietnam War of the late 1960s and early 1970s. His sangha, or spiritual community, was devastated by bombings and guerilla fighting, but they maintained non-violent efforts to cultivate peace. On a trip to the United States in 1966, Thich Nhat Hahn, called for a unilateral cease-fire, and was told that he would not be allowed back into his country. Instead, he found asylum in France, and worked to establish dharma centers there. In1967, Dr. Martin Luther King, Jr. nominated him for the Nobel Peace Prize.

Whenever I think about this story, I am humbled. It may be hard enough for any of us to stop ourselves from yelling angry words at a person who cuts us off in traffic. But this man saw people he loved, gentle people who lived and worshipped in the forests, killed by bands of guerillas. Despite all of it, he was able to keep his equanimity. Someone else might have picked up arms and searched for the murderers to even the score. But he lost fiends, his community, and his country, all so people of all nations would not have to keep dying. In January of 2005, nearly four decades later, he finally returned to his homeland, reuniting with his people and his sangha.

If we want peace—in our lives, in our stories, or in our relationships—we must aspire to the same kind of bravery. We must be unflinching, and dedicated to telling the truth. This is not to say that we must find ourselves in a war zone before we're capable of talking about peace, but that we must get beyond its outward signifiers. It's fine to wear a peace sign on your t-shirt or go to a peace march, because these things are galvanizing. Communities, by their nature, are larger than the individual. But our stories come from a far deeper place within us, and we must strive to access that part of us, knowing that the war within us will not know the sweet mercy of peace unless we take the time to negotiate with our darker forces. More on this later.

Love

Love has got to be one of the most loaded words in the entire English language. When you read it or hear it, your mind may be filled all at once with hearts and flowers, chubby little cupids with their arrows poised to fire. You may see images of chocolate hearts, or red and pink Valentine's Day cards. Right?

We may think of love, first and foremost, as a way of desiring and being desired. We may see depictions of love on television, or read about them in magazines and books, and wonder if our lives could ever be as full as the people living in those pictures, or between those lines of type. If we have a spiritual practice, we may even think about other types of love from time to time.

But think about this for a minute. As defined by the American Heritage Dictionary, love is, "A deep, tender, ineffable feeling of affection and solicitude toward a person, such as that arising from kinship, recognition of attractive qualities, or a sense of underlying oneness." I don't know about you, but to me, this sounds exactly like the thing I aim for when I tell a story.

Just off the top of my head, here are just a few of the ways we express love, probably every day:

- Love of closeness and/or sex

- Love of spirituality or religion

- Love of pets

- Love of humanity

- Love of children

- Love of language

- Love of food

- Love of music

- Love of family
- Love of country or homeland
- Love of volunteering
- Love of money
- Love of dance
- Love of self
- Love of painting
- Love of communication
- Love of chocolate

We'll make our own lists later, as part of this week's exercise. This list is just to get you thinking along these lines. Romantic and sexual love are both wonderful things, but they must never supercede or become more important than other types of love. To give in to that way of thinking is to become a mark, for someone to sell you their story, of what love is, or should be. Only we determine what our love stories will look like, and only we choose who to share them with, or whether to share them at all.

The first step is to clarify what we mean when we say the word love. It's a term that's often confused with others that mean almost the same thing. Affection, for example, is a gentler word, which evokes a tender response to someone or something. Devotion is almost chaste and selfless in its meaning. Fondness is a little warmer, and implies a real need to connect with another person. But many of us may confuse love with infatuation, which is really a sort of silly or immature attraction, lasting no longer than the convenience of having the object of infatuation around. When something better comes along, we assume that this sort of love will simply evaporate.

There is an urban legend that Eskimos have more than a

hundred words to describe snow, because they are constantly surrounded by it (in actuality, the Inuit people, commonly called Eskimos, have about a dozen of these words, about the same number as the English language). The logic goes that, since snow is a huge part of the Eskimo's life, he needs that many words to shade his meaning.

We might think about the word love in much the same way. If we are constantly surrounded by it, as the Inuit are by snow, why are we so obsessed with it? Wouldn't it have become mundane by now? Rather, I believe that we have so many words to shade the meaning of love because of its importance in our lives.

Let's face it. We could all live very long and relatively happy lives without experiencing romantic or sexual love. But we could simply not exist without other types of love. One of these is the love of our parents and protectors, the ones who cared for us when we were completely defenseless. Another is love of humanity, and that common cord that binds all of us into a shared fate, regardless of whether we know one another personally.

Recording and sharing stories is one way of cementing that bond that connects us. When we tell a story that's personal to us and our experience, we are assuming our portion of the space on the planet. Far from being selfish or demanding, this is a subtle but powerful way of being seen and heard by others, and of offering ourselves to the human conversation. Who is to say that reading a story written by you cannot heal a person living in Turkey, or China, or Alaska? Who is to say that hearing a story read out loud by you cannot make people in France pull together, or people in Africa cry, or people in Texas laugh out loud? As many times as we have been stirred or moved to action by the words of others is the exact number of times it's possible for us to do the same for them.

The secret is in understanding the concept of love that connects us. It is not love in an insubstantial or infatuated way, because sometimes love is not that simple. It is not conditional love, which evaporates when someone says or does something we don't agree with. Rather, it's love of ourselves and our stories directed outward, so that others may hear and receive the stories the way we meant them, as gifts. By constantly sending and receiving stories like this, we strengthen the chains in the human conversation. We build bridges of understanding, one story at a time. We extend ourselves in greeting, and deepen our understanding of those who may be like us in the tiniest ways of all.

Understanding

It may be easy for us to say we understand someone or something. We gather little clues in that person's speech or actions, and believe we have him or her pegged. Having lived in New York City for many years, I thought I had the people who lived there pegged pretty well, until I saw the television footage from the 9/11 attacks.

I had always felt at home with some of the more loud-mouthed of New Yorkers, believing that way was a little more honest than most. I have been part of many rush hour crowds shoving too many bodies into subways trains, or been pushed out of the way on a crowded sidewalk. In a way, I was used to it.

On 9/11/01, I was living in Los Angeles. A friend called early, around 8:00 am, and told my husband to turn on the television. We stood in the living room, holding hands, crying and not knowing what to do. I thought of all the friends I knew who worked in that area of Manhattan. I picked up the phone and started dialing, but got the same busy signal as everyone else.

We stayed home from work, moving around the house

silently. The footage on television didn't get any better. In the farthest reaches of downtown, people looked like ghosts, wearing business attire that had been coated with gray ash. Some ran, stumbling and being helped up by others. Others supported people they didn't even know by the shoulders, taking their briefcases or purses and helping them to safety. There were no loud-mouths or opinion-sharers, no shoving to get a better seat on the subway. I saw grace on that day in New York, and it still moves me.

The day after 9/11, I realized I didn't really understand the place I had lived for almost a decade. I didn't really understand its people, or know what they were capable of. I was glad to know that even in the most self-involved seeming people, there is a place that can still be touched.

Understanding may be such a hard thing to practice, but we must realize that even when we think we have someone pegged, we don't. Even the most hardened person has something they love. Our stories can help break down the walls we build between true understanding and what we think we know. They can show us another race, another family structure, another sexuality. They can show us a place thousands of miles away from where we grew up, and what it feels like in the skin of someone living next door.

Bravery is the key to achieving true understanding. We must learn to trust our intentions towards others, and our experiences with them. But we must also not become too enamored of our senses. Though they help us create a picture of our reality, without asking them to pass through an emotional inspection process, we cut ourselves off from others. Being able to open ourselves fully, and to suspend our disbelief a little, allows us to let others into our lives through the medium of their stories. In the words of the movie Crash, "You may think you know, but you have no idea."

Meditation:

This week, we'll focus our meditation exercise on awakening love in our lives. We'll try to get in touch with that particular brand of love that connects rather than divides, and helps us to realize that, as the characters in our own stories, we are only as good as the love we give to ourselves and others.

In order to do this, we're going to do a version of a Tibetan practice called lojong mediation which, loosely translated, means "giving and receiving." By taking on the suffering of others symbolically, we awaken to a kind of love that truly connects us.

You may notice more changes come over you this week, most likely pertaining to your relationships with others. You may find that you want to reach out a little more, or that you want to contact someone you haven't thought about in ages. This is a natural part of the process, as I have found. If you have few satisfying relationships, you may want to think about strategizing to bring new people into your life.

Your work so far has brought you to a place of great power. Now more than ever before, you may be starting to notice your life in a brand new way. Positives may be standing out more, as well as negatives. Now that you can see them more clearly, it's much easier to take appropriate action.

- Go into your private meditation space and close the door. As always, please make sure you have about thirty minutes of uninterrupted time for your work. You may need a little more time for processing your feelings, and recording your experience in your notebook or using your tape recorder.

- Bring your body into your preferred meditation posture, on a cushion with your legs crossed, or seated in a chair, with your feet flat on the floor. Keep the rest of your body straight but not rigid, trying to strike a balance between holding yourself too loose or too tight.

- Relax each of your body parts, trying to become aware of the way you are put together. Once you have the posture you want, try to relax into it as much as you can. Feel your body as you get in touch with what your mind is doing.

- Focus on your breath as it moves in and out of your body, filling you with air and then exhaling. Let your mind wander as you orient yourself in this practice. Feel your heart rate slowing. Begin your Base Practice, labeling your thought by saying "thinking" to yourself when you notice yourself having them. Let your thoughts leave you without judging them, or yourself. Take five full breaths here.

- Spend the next few breaths connecting each of your five senses to your meditation. Move through the senses in whichever order seems right for you today, feeling that part of the body and labeling the sense it corresponds with. For example, become aware of your eyes and their function in your life, saying "seeing" to yourself. It's important to understand how each of these senses helps you to interpret the world.

- After you have connected all five of your senses, take five more full breaths here. In order to begin the practice of "giving and receiving," we'll need to pick a person to work with. You might choose someone you know who could use some help in some way. This person may be a friend, a member of your family, or a stranger you see every day when you're walking to work. You need only to be able to hold this person's face in your mind. Some people may even wish to work with themselves, and this is fine, too.

- Keep breathing, while you hold this person's face in your

mind. Try to think of what might be causing this person to suffer. When you breathe in, feel whatever that is leaving them and (symbolically only) being taken on by you. Some teachers describe the suffering as "hot, black, or smoky" in nature. You may give it any characteristics that help you get in touch with what this person might be going through at this time.

- When you breathe out, send this person whatever you feel will help. It could be medicine, if someone is sick, or a cool bath, if that person has a fever. It could be an ice cream cone, if that person is depressed, or a great new job, if someone is unemployed. See as much of it in your mind's eye as you can. Maybe you see the person you're working with picking up the phone and accepting a great job offer. Teachers like to give this part of the meditation qualities such as, "cool, quenching, or clear" in nature.

- Keep going like this for a few breaths, sending the person you're working with all the comfort he or she might need. Now widen it out a little bit, sending that same sense of comfort, or that same individual remedy, to everyone on your block, or everyone in your town. See how it affects the people you're touching with your practice. Notice how they react.

- Widen your meditation as wide as you can today, to your city, your state, your country, your hemisphere, or even the entire world. In your mind, label this "love." Remember that it's not a contest, to see how far we can go, but rather a means of connecting our good intentions with others. However far you can go today is great. The most important thing to remember is that we are getting a three-dimensional picture of what love looks like. Know that this is accessible to you at any time.

- How does that feel? Take a moment, while still breathing evenly, to look into your emotions. What has been activated for you? Have any memories come up? Take a few breaths here, noticing and validating your feelings.

- Now take a moment to see how your body was affected by this meditation. Does your body feel any differently now than when we first began? Where are you holding tension at this moment? Take five full breaths here, allowing your body to relax as much as it can right now.

- If the Little Destroyers have come into your meditation, or begin to harp on something unique to you, try to release them with your out breath. Some of my students have reported that the Little Destroyers like to say things like, "You'll get cancer if you take on Gill's pain," or "Don't you know you're only hurting yourself by doing this?" This is a symbolic exercise only, to get in touch with the concept of love. It is not humanly possible to "catch" someone else's cancer in this way. Let the Little Destroyers go. Keep breathing.

- Return to your Base Practice, labeling your thoughts to yourself, as you become aware of them. Take five full breaths here, knowing you have contacted a universal kind of love, perhaps for the first time. Let your mind clear and allow yourself to come out of the meditation.

Exercise:

Take your time as you come back into normal consciousness. Sometimes, people need a bit more time to refocus after doing this style of meditation. When you feel ready to do so, record the experiences you had during the meditation session. How did it feel to work with the person you chose? What changes did you notice about yourself as you took on the pain of that person? Did the pain change while you were working with it, to something you might not have expected?

Did you notice a change in that person's demeanor as

you took the suffering away and replaced it with whatever was needed? What signs did you get from that person, to show that he or she was appreciative? If you chose to work with yourself, what changes did you notice in your emotional state, or in your body?

Did you recognize any fears ? Any unfulfilled needs, or abandoned goals?

And finally, what did it feel like to construct this three-dimensional picture of love? Did it change how you think about that word? Did it make you feel powerful, knowing that you can access this deeply human love at any time, for yourself or others?

Write down what you saw, and how it made you feel. If there was a conversation between you and the person you chose to work with, try to recall that as best you can, and record it in your notebook or using your recorder. There is no need to edit your work, or try to make it sound pretty. Just try to capture the authentic nature of what happened, along with the actual words and thoughts that might have been going through your mind at the time.

If the Little Destroyers made an appearance, also record what they said to you, or how they tried to persuade you that awakening to love was not a good idea. Many times, I have heard students say that their Little Destroyers tried to convince them that taking on other people's suffering would only increase their own. What do you think of that, now that you have been through the process for yourself?

When you have recorded everything you can remember about your meditation session, take a moment to think about the concept of love. What do you think about that word now? Take a moment to free-write (or free-speak) on that word, that concept. What does it bring to mind now? Use descriptive words you may not have associated with love before. Instead of "candy," maybe try "hot dog," if you

118

have a wonderful, loving memory of spending a day at the ballpark with your father as a child. Instead of "flowers," try "oranges," if you can remember a beautiful summer day eating oranges with your best friend, and letting the juice drip down your giggling faces.

Take a moment here to let your mind draw some quick conclusions about the concept of love. Let them come forward freely, without judgement or interpretation. At first, they may not seem to make sense. But oftentimes, in order to be truly authentic, our memories have to bypass the gatekeepers of reason at the edge of our consciousness. Let it rip.

Lastly, check in with your body. How is it feeling, now that you have experienced "sending and receiving"? Are memories seemingly lodged in one part of your body or another, as evidenced by a certain stiffness or knotted feeling? Do you have any internal issues, such as a stomachache or nausea?

Connect with your expectations of what you thought you would experience, and measure them against what you did experience. Can you see that connecting with this type of love may not be at all like going on a date, or getting married, but that it is the most connective type of love, shared by every single person on the planet?

In the next few chapters, we will learn to connect this type of love to the people in our stories, whether that person is us or someone else. Having the ability to love and forgive your main character for being human and fallible is one of the strongest tools a storyteller can have. In this way, we do not shy away from unattractive behaviors simply because we don't like them. We are able to simultaneously see the ugliness of what is happening and still love the character (even if it's us!) for being human.

During the week, try to do this meditation exercise every day. You may choose to work with the same person, or a different person each day, if you wish. You may choose to work with yourself at least once, to see how that feels.

If you can, try to widen whatever you're sending out to include all readers of this book, who may have more in common with you than you might think. Think of yourselves as a large family, of members still waiting to meet one another.

Follow-Up:

For each day of the week, make sure to do your "sending and receiving" meditation practice, making time for yourself as needed. You may feel crunched by the demands of your days, but there is always a little time to be found somewhere, even if you have to get a little tough in demanding it.

You are growing and developing as a storyteller each week that you continue this practice. During the next four weeks, we will take what we have been uncovering in ourselves and start to give it form. Please continue to notice changes in your emotional body as well as your physical body as these things come up, whether in a mediation session or in your daily life.

As you continue to awaken love in your daily meditation sessions, try to bring this practice "off the mat," or into your walking-around life. If a conflict arises at work, or with a friend, can you call upon these techniques to awaken feelings of love for that person, before getting angry and saying something you might later regret? If not, don't worry. It is a practice, and will probably become stronger the more it is reinforced.

If you would like an additional challenge, try working with someone entirely neutral, such as a stranger, or even a person you find very difficult to deal with, or someone towards whom you have a lot of animosity. If you feel you want to give it a try, it can be very rewarding, in terms of what we notice about ourselves, and how we tend to close up around people we find hard to get along with. People like these may become characters in your future stories, so it's best to try working with them as soon as you are able to.

See how love inspires and informs your stories, whether they are the ones you tell to others about the adventures you have, or whether they are the ones you have made up about others, such as the reason behind your co-worker Ursula's short temper. Begin to see how your feelings towards another person may regulate the love you allow yourself to feel for that person. There is no need to change this fact. Just seeing it and acknowledging it is enough.

Try to notice how you share love with others in your daily life. Are you a demonstrative person, or someone who tends to hang back? How do you usually show people you care for them? Do certain people inspire rare and indulgent gestures and, if so, why do you think that is?

Do you have a desire to have love, but a fear of showing it, or even talking about it openly? These seem to be very common concerns among human beings, so you are certainly not alone. If fears come up while doing these practices, refer back to the meditation from last week, along with the notes you took at that time.

Remind yourself that you can always return to the Base Practice, breathing slowly and deeply, and releasing your thoughts by labeling them and allowing them to leave you on the out breath.

Next week, we'll use the tools we've learned in order to get out of the way of telling and sharing our stories. By refusing to control every aspect of our lives, we silently agree to do the same with our stories. By extending the love we have awakened towards ourselves and others, we create a safe environment to be truly human. And by offering up our unique qualities, we change the world a little at a time.

7 Getting Out of the Way

"Storytelling reveals meaning without committing the error of defining it."

— Hannah Arendt

You've passed the halfway mark on your journey towards waking up to your stories, and are coming into the home stretch. You've seen how silence equals complicity when it comes to storytelling, in the mass media, and in your own lives, where others may be left to create and maintain your personal mythologies. Slowly but surely, you are peeling back the veils from your eyes. Without these veils, you will see yourselves and others, not to mention the characters in your stories, with more tolerance and insight.

Let's take a minute to check in from last week:

- Did you get to do your meditation exercises every day?

- Were you able to do the "sending and receiving" practice as well?

- Who did you choose to work with? Is this person close to you?

- How did it feel to take on that person's suffering, and be able to offer something tangible to make that person feel better?

- Were you able to extend this "sending and receiving" outward, to include your street, your town or city, your country, or even the entire planet?

- Were you able to extend this practice to a neutral person, or to a person you may find difficult or downright annoying?

- What changes did you notice in your emotions before and after you did this?

- What changes did you notice in your body before and after you did this?

- Has this exercise changed the way you think about love?

- If so, how has your view changed?

- Were you able to extend this practice of awakening love into your daily life?

- If so, what were your experiences?

- Did any fears come up, as you explored feeling and showing love?

- What did you notice about the way you show others you care about them?

- Have you noticed that you are less likely to take things personally as a result of this practice?

- Finally, have you experienced anything different about the way you view yourself and your work going forward?

Take some time to record the answers to these questions in your notebook or into your tape recorder. Then look inside yourself, to see how you're feeling. What emotions are you having right now? What physical feelings are accompanying these emotions? Ground yourself by understanding exactly what's happening for you at this moment, and knowing that whatever it is, it's absolutely right.

Thought Into Action

We've explored the fears we all have when we set out to tell our stories, and have started to adopt strategies to deal with them. We have begun to notice these fears as simply more thoughts that move through our busy minds. This process is more than half of the battle when it comes to waking up to our stories, and cultivating the fearlessness required to share them with others.

Now what's needed is action.

Fear is an internal mechanism. As we've discussed, it developed in humans as a response to the threats in our immediate environment. But fear can manifest outwardly as well, and when it does, we need external actions to meet the fears head-on. This is the process of turning thought into action, or getting out of the way.

Learning how to do this will prepare us for turning our internal practices, which we have been staying with diligently all these weeks, into external action, in the form of writing down or speaking our stories. Though meditation may make some of you feel spacey or out of it, as I know it does me sometimes, we will learn how to manage the space between meditation and "off the mat practice," when it's time to deal with the challenges and joys of the external world. In time, your mind will be tamed, and yet somehow sharpened, as a result of these experiences.

The Last Vestiges of Fear

Some fears, you may notice, want to hang around longer than others. By now, you may be very good at recognizing and thwarting the Little Destroyers before they can get their hooks into your mind. But there is another layer that lurks beneath those fears, which I call the Underneath. Sounds like a Stephen King novel, right?

The Underneath is the part of you that is so old, you may not remember installing it as part of your belief system. And because of that, it's very hard to see or discern, no less dislodge. As an infant, you may have measured your mother's responses to your cries within seconds, coming to a decision about your own worth if your expectations were not met. Psychologists now believe that all of us are capable of making these types of pre-verbal decisions that stick around with us well into our adult years.

One of these is Candace Pert, who holds a Ph.D. in pharmacology from Johns Hopkins University and teaches "new paradigm" healing at the Georgetown University Medical School, where she is a professor of Physiology and Biophysics. Her work is one of the first government-funded research projects designed to connect the functions of the body and the mind. Of course, each of these areas has been studied extensively on its own, yielding thousands of articles and findings. But few researchers of Western, or allopathic, medicine have delved into the relationship between the body and the mind before now.

Pert has found that our memories become stored, in measurable ways, in our bodies — in our muscles, our tissues, and our skin. We "remember" pleasurable or traumatic experiences we've had and react accordingly, even if none of this is available to our conscious minds. To us, it may all seem like we're just being who we are.

Because this is so, it's important to recognize the existence of the Underneath, even though we may choose different ways of coping with it. One way that I have found of keeping it preoccupied is to reawaken the sense of play.

A Sense of Play

For me, this concept has always seemed silly, in a way. Though certain parts of the psychological and metaphysical communities use time-tested techniques for dealing with abuse and "inner child" issues, and find that their work is helpful to some, forcing oneself to recapture the joy we're all supposed to feel while playing always seemed a bit forced and militaristic to me. "Go outside and play!" I hear my inner voice saying, with a none-too-subtle shove. "Hurry up! Enjoy yourself!"

Instead, I try to think of "play" as a sixth sense, rather than forcing myself to be playful when I don't feel that way. People talk about psychic ability as a sixth sense, so why not "play"? Or, if you have already manifested some psychic ability, perhaps "play" can be your seventh sense. In any event, sixth or seventh senses do not have to be engendered. They are always there, waiting for us to be open enough to take advantage of the information they have to share with us. If we can sense things that are about to happen, why can't we actually set them in motion ourselves?

Play has been the way I can connect with people in my life, or the characters in my writing, even when I'm personally not feeling that way. Actors have to connect with all sorts of emotions they may not be actually feeling while appearing in a stage play. In the same way, storytellers must be able to connect with a wide range of emotions, in the way they capture stories and as they tell them to others.

Shyness, conditioning, and other factors may come up as warnings that the Underneath is at work. Stop right there, they say, in order to keep us from recording our stories or,

God forbid, sharing them with other people. We may be so close to allowing ourselves the human connection and healing that comes with this process, but emotionally, we just can't go another step. It's the presence of the Underneath that keeps us from taking that final action, that final step that could, quite literally, dissolve the rest of the fear in its tracks.

Of course, if your fear reveals something traumatic, it's important to enlist the help of a trained professional to develop coping strategies and greater emotional health. Working with the mind in meditation can always bring up things you may not have been expecting, so be vigilant. This can't be underestimated. Only you will know when you are experiencing more than you can handle. If scary dreams arise for you, it may be time to ask for help.

With that being said, I have found that developing a sense of play can keep The Underneath at bay long enough for you to turn your thoughts into action, especially when it comes to waking up to your stories.

Living Outside Time

What's needed is the ability to reconnect with that childlike part of you that refused to acknowledge time. Caught up in your reverie, in nature or a game, you had no worries, no cares, no past and no future. It was all about the moment at hand, just like you are when you're inside your meditation practice.

People try all kinds of ways to achieve this state, employing drugs, alcohol, exercise, strict ascetic diets, or other methods. Many equate it with a kind of bliss, when things were simpler, and none of us had to worry about the mundane things of life. For us, there were no bills, relationships, or jobs. There was only the moment, stretched out in front of us, pregnant with possibility.

But getting caught up in not having responsibility only deepens our suffering. It is not the lack of having to perform adult tasks that formed the nucleus of our joy at that childhood moment, it was our ability to live outside time. This is a trait we learned to have as soon as we began hearing stories. If we think back to the stories that have stuck with us all these years, chances are there was an element of living outside time in them. Perhaps a hero had to fight a dragon much larger than himself, or a heroine had to cross enormous distances with the help of her seven league boots.

As small beings, we needed these assurances, that despite our size, we could have an affect on the world. It doesn't change much as we become adults. Though we exist in larger bodies, and have learned how to affect the world enough that we can make a living, feed ourselves, and establish relationships, we still want to believe that there are magical "levelers" that help us to achieve tasks that we find daunting or impossible to consider. These give us hope that we can play on the same field as those we perceive as more powerful.

We still need these small assurances, and the best way to reconnect with them is to learn to live outside time in small and controlled ways. In this way, we do not disturb the instances in our lives when we need to be extremely aware and present, such as when caring for children, while driving, or at our jobs.

If you have children, or are inclined to try this on your own, you can start with playing games. My husband and I like to invite people over for board game nights sometimes. It has an old-fashioned, family feel to it, but you might be surprised at what comes up for you and your guests if you decide to host one of these evenings yourself.

Engaging in activities with which we have very old associations, such as board games, jumping rope, hopscotch, or even raking leaves, can help to release old memories. Since, as Candace Pert's research shows, our memories are stored in the tissues and muscles of our bodies, moving those tissues and muscles can help to jog our memories loose. If you take part in an exercise program now, or practice yoga or tai chi, you may have already noticed that your mind becomes simultaneously still and observant during your practice, and immediately thereafter.

But releasing the memories is only part of the battle. It's so easy, in our busy world, to immediately forget what we've just uncovered. Writing the memories down, or speaking them into a tape recorder, with as much detail as possible, helps us to preserve them for use in future stories. What are the colors that set the scenes we remember? What is the temperature? How are people dressed in this memory? Who are they, and how do they speak to one another? Why are you gathered together in this memory? When is it taking place – can you recall the year, or events that frame this time of your life?

This act of writing down what we have released through the act of play lets us become a camera in our own lives. Once we have allowed a memory to pass between our unconscious and conscious awareness, we turn toward it and click! We have preserved it, connecting with that childlike part of us that loved to play while still retaining our adult dignity and concerns. The part of us that is like a camera can freeze moments in time, and teach us to live outside of it, for moments or hours at a time.

Meditation:

In this week's meditation exercise, we'll work on getting out of the way, so our worries and anxieties don't prevent the rich stuff of memory to present itself for our stories. For right now, we won't try to contact specific memories, just remove obstacles to them coming forward. In the next few weeks, we'll supplement this practice with additional prompts to help you begin to structure these memories into coherent stories.

The most important part of this week's practice, therefore, requires that we become even less judgmental of the thoughts and feelings that might come up for us. We must develop a kind of mental dexterity that allows us to validate and honor our feelings while being able to step aside, quickly and decisively.

While learning this practice, you may experience yourself moving in and out of time more readily, and being able to go a bit deeper each time you try it. It may make you feel spacey, until you get used to it. As always, try to leave yourself at least thirty minutes to engage in the meditation practice, as well as a few more minutes to record your experiences on paper or using the tape recorder.

Telling stories is not just a matter of repeating words that have been passed down from generation to generation. It is an incredibly conscious act, which stands as a connector between our past and our future. Our stories, then, become the bridge that takes us from here to there.

- Go to your meditation spot, making sure that you have the time in your schedule to do some great work. Close the door, and make sure that you will not be disturbed for about thirty minutes, give or take. Make sure you have your notebook and a pen or pencil, if you are writing down your memories, or your tape recorder, if you are recording your experiences this way.

- Arrange your body into your preferred meditation posture, whether you're more comfortable sitting in a cross-legged position or seated in a chair. Remember to have your feet flat on the floor if you've decided to sit in a chair, since we're trying to establish a connection with the ground, which always supports our meditation posture. Hold your body with dignity and balance, establishing harmony between floppy and ramrod straight.

- Become aware of your breath as it moves in and out

130

of your body. Don't try to breathe at a certain rate, or control what your body wants to do right now. Rather, feel yourself as a vessel, and see if you can get in touch with the feeling of "being breathed."

- Now become aware of the muscles in your body, taking a minute to move your awareness to any place that might feel tight or painful. Relax each of your body parts, moving from top to bottom or from the bottom up. If there is a place in your body that doesn't want to relax, acknowledge that and move on. Once you have relaxed all that you can, feel your way into the posture, making any necessary adjustments.

- Bring your awareness to the thoughts moving through your mind and begin to label them by saying, "thinking," silently to yourself. Continue with your Base Practice as you feel your heart rate slowing and your breath coming easily, with less effort. Let your thoughts be released as they ride the out breath. Take five full inhalations and exhalations here.

- Now connect each of your five senses to your meditation practice, taking time to label each sense silently, to yourself. Feel the parts of your body that bring you important sensory information. Understand how each of them helps to connect you with the world you live in.

- When you have connected each of your senses to your practice, go back to your Base Practice and take five more breaths here. As we endeavor to get out of the way, we'll need to choose one important fear or worry to work with. You may choose the fear we worked with back in Chapter 5, or another worry that has nagged you throughout this program of waking up to your stories. You will know it when you have it, because it will suddenly "feel right. "

- As you hold this worry or fear in your mind, notice how your body may have changed. Do you notice any tension constricting any part of your body? Do you notice anything different about the thoughts you're having now, as opposed to a few minutes ago? Have any strong feelings come up for you? Notice these things and then return to your breath, holding this worry or fear at the center of your awareness.

- Now visualize a large box beside you. If you are seated on a cushion or on the floor, make the box about the same size you are when you're seated. If you're sitting in a chair, make your box about the same height as your knees, or maybe a little bit taller than that. Your box can be uniquely your own, whether it's made of standard brown cardboard or solid gold. I like to visualize mine in a kind of purple brocade, so it has a sense of elegance to it.

- When you have your box perfectly visualized in your mind, transfer your worry or fear into the box. It will move through the air, very gently, and be set down inside the box. You may even think about yourself watching over the side of the box as you place your worry inside. If your worry or fear seems to have a personality, or certain reactive qualities, notice how it reacts to being set inside this box.

- Retain your gentleness as you return to your breath, watching your thoughts as they arise and labeling them with the out breath. Give yourself a few breaths to notice whether any other strong fears or worries come up for you. These may be some of the ones we've covered, or they may be entirely new worries. Some of them may not even seem to make sense. Regardless, please take the time to carefully transfer them into your box.

- When you have transferred all of your worries and fears into the box, close each of the four flaps, replace the top, or close the lid, depending on the type of box you may have visualized. I like to tie mine up with a luxurious velvet ribbon, taking the kind of care I would if I were wrapping a gorgeous present for someone I love. Know that you are able to access these fears and worries as you need to. For now, it's safe to keep them here.

- Visualize yourself placing the box on the top shelf of your closet, or in a clean, dry place in your garage. Try not to place it so far back that you can't see it on a day-to-day basis, but rather in plain sight. That way, you will always be reminded of its presence in your life.

- Return to your Base Practice, watching your breath and noticing any thoughts or feelings that may have come up for you. Stay like this for five breaths, calmly allowing yourself to be in this moment, without rushing forward into the next.

- Now see yourself in a forest, playing hide and go seek with a friend or sibling. The weather is comfortable, and you have no worries about bills or a career. Nothing can touch you. You are running, without cares, laughing. The sun is streaming down on your hair and feels warm along your back. You are determined not to be found by the person looking for you, so you can win a prize. Who is chasing you? Where do you decide to hide? How does your body feel as you crouch into your hiding place? What do you do so you won't make a sound and give yourself away?

- Hold this image in your mind as you notice the thoughts moving through your mind, and the feelings they may be triggering. How has your body reacted to this visualization? Can you feel anything welling inside you? Take a few breaths here, taking a moment to validate whatever has come up.

- Now take a moment to see if any memories have been activated. Does the feeling of running release something in you? The act of hiding? The hope of wining a prize if you do something very well? Notice whatever is most prevalent for you, without judging or trying to analyze it. Also take notice of any tension you may be holding in your body now, especially if it is different from when we began the meditation practice.

• Return to your Base Practice, breathing and labeling your thoughts as they arise in your mind. Take five complete breaths here, letting your mind return to its normal rhythms. Allow your mind to release any leftover worries or fears that may have accumulated since you stored yours away, and come out of the meditation. Give yourself a few minutes for your mind to clear.

Exercise:

After you have returned to normal consciousness, spend a few minutes reviewing your experience in the meditation. Your non-meditating mind will come into focus as you do this. Now record your experiences, using your notebook or tape recorder.

Were you able to identify one particularly strong fear or worry which causes you to stand in the way? What did it feel like to hold that fear or worry in your mind, and then transfer it into the box you visualized? Was that transfer accompanied by any additional sensations in your body? If so, were they centralized in any one area?

When the meditation shifted to the game of hide-and-seek, what did you experience? Who were you playing with, and what did you look like? About how old were you? What sensations were moving through your body? What feelings did you have? And were any memories activated, from an earlier time in your life?

Did you notice any additional fears or worries come up after you had played your game of hide-and-seek? If so, were you able to work with them? Did the Little Destroyers make

134

an appearance, to dampen your play? If so, you might try inviting them to play along with you next time.

Did you notice any telltale signs that you were dealing with the Underneath? Did you feel like you were ready to go to the edge of yourself to find your stories, and get almost there, but not quite? What stories did you tell yourself to stop going that last step? What dangers did you perceive were lurking there, just under the surface?

Lastly, were you able to achieve the sensation of being a camera, and being able to freeze time? If so, how did that feel to you? Was it scary or pleasurable? Helpful or frustrating?

Write down what you experienced in your meditation session, along with the feelings you had during the session. If you were able to dislodge a memory, please take the time to record as much of it as you can, including little sensory details like smells, sights, sounds, tastes, etc. If you are speaking into a tape recorder, don't try to make your words sound pretty. Just let them come out in a rush, without any mental editing. Try to capture the feeling of being in your body at that time of your life as authentically as you can.

If the Little Destroyers of the Underneath made appearances, try to remember what they felt like, both in your body as the adult you are now, as well as the person you were at the time of the memory. What signs did you receive that you were not supposed to go another step towards discovering this deeper part of yourself? What threats did you perceive?

Once you have finished the process of recording your experiences, spend a few minutes just relaxing into the present moment. This meditation is sometimes particularly insightful for some, and may require a little more time before you're ready to come back into the "real" world.

How did you feel about yourself and the work you're

doing at this moment? What images come to mind when you think about taking the time to discover this very old part of yourself? How did it feel to connect with old memories in this way? Does it give you renewed hope for your personal development as well as the development of your storytelling work?

Then take a moment to check back in with your body. Are you feeling tired? Relaxed? Apprehensive? Shocked? Locate any sources of tension or trepidation. Did your memory seem to come out of a certain area of your body, and if so, where? Look deeply into the person you are right now, both body and soul.

Did you have any expectations about this meditation? If you did, were your expectations met, or did you have a completely different experience from the one you thought you'd have? Can you see how this practice of unearthing memories can help you as you wake up to your stories?

During the week, make sure to participate in the meditation exercise every day. You may find that, in the spirit of awakening play, you want to try other games, or attempt to connect with other people and memories from your past. Have fun with it. Explore how this meditation makes you feel as a person and as a storyteller. Enjoy the rich material it provides for you.

Hold onto the sense of play in everything you do. Even challenging situations can be mitigated with a healthy dose of humor. When your mind is relaxed enough to play like this, you may find that insights normally "withheld" from you come forward more readily.

Follow-Up:

For each day of the week, be sure to do the meditation practice involving your worries or fears as they are placed into a box of your creation. Then shift the meditation to a game of hopscotch, hide-and-seek, or another childhood game. Though it may seem silly in the scope of our worldly demands, taking the time to connect with yourself in this way brings benefits ranging from general relaxation and stress reduction to the retrieval of dear childhood memories for storytelling purposes. Make sure to record your experiences after each session, and note any changes to your emotional or physical body after the session has taken place.

As with last week's practice, try to take your experiences off the mat. In your daily life, take stock of your sense of play. Do you approach your days with a playful air, or is everything always heavy and serious? If you are always serious, does it have to be that way, or could a little calculated play help you and the others around you enjoy your time on the planet a little more? The challenge lies in trying to instill this sense of play as an additional sense, so it doesn't feel external or unnatural. Over time, this will happen, if practiced enough. Play will become one of the ways in which you access the external world, like inhaling to smell, or opening your eyes to see.

If you have some board games shoved way back in a closet, get them out and see if you still like to play. You may find a likeminded group of friends who want to join in the fun. Scrabble is great for starting conversations and developing your vocabulary.

If board games aren't your thing, think about what kinds of games you liked as a child. Do you still do any of them? If not, could some form of physical exercise, such as running, substitute for the joy of not having anywhere to be? Try playing games on the Internet with complete strangers, or write about playing games as a child. All of these are ways of getting you in touch with that sense of play that kept you outside time when you were small.

If you'd like an additional challenge, try taking a camera out into the street, or around with you on your daily rounds.

It doesn't have to be a fancy camera. Even a disposable one is fine for this exercise. All day long, whenever an image catches your eye, snap a picture. Don't think about why, per se, just let yourself gravitate towards the things that seem important to you.

Develop the pictures as soon as you can. If it takes you all week to shoot one roll of film, that's fine, but it would be great if you could have the pictures developed before the last day of the week, if possible.

On the last day of your week, after your meditation practice, think about how telling stories is like playing games. By now, you will have had six days of reconnecting with your sense of play. Do you prefer physical games, or mental ones? Have you managed to connect with something you used to love to do?

Then spend a few minutes writing about or speaking about why you were attracted to each image you chose. Just a word, or a few sentences is fine. They don't even have to be complete sentences. Fragments are great, too. This will give you even more insight into the types of stories you might be inclined to tell, as well as how your storytelling "voice" is unique to your inner world.

See how connections inform your stories, and how connections are bolstered by the sense of play. See how instilling that sense of play not only makes life more pleasurable, but arms you with the tools you need to keep the Underneath busy with diversions. Share your newfound sense of play with others in your life, noticing how this makes you feel. Does it open you up, and make you feel closer to the people in your life? Or does it frighten you, to become this vulnerable in front of others?

Remember, there are no right answers. It's only crucial to be honest with yourself, no matter what's coming up for you. These tools are preparing you to wake up to the stories living

138

Wake Up to Your Stories

inside you, and will make it easier to share them with others in time, even if you're a very shy person now.

In the next chapter, we will use this practice of unearthing memories by getting in touch with the concept of impermanence. Everyone we know, from our friends to our relatives and co-workers, have to die. We will die, and the characters we create will also have to die one day, unless we're writing some form of science fiction.

This can become a reason to mourn our short time on earth, or it can provide very fertile material for a storyteller. When we realize that there has to be an end to everything we put our minds to, we deepen the meaning behind our actions. And whether we're drawn to telling stories for personal expression or family reasons, we can make the mysterious manifest simply by telling our stories to one other person.

8 Ghosts

"Madame, all stories, if continued far enough, end in death, and he is no true-story teller who would keep that from you."

— Ernest Hemingway

Congratulations on making it through another week of waking up to your stories! Your work in dealing with fears, worries, and the Underneath has all been fruitful for you, I trust, and helpful when coupled with a burgeoning sense of play. As you move through these meditations and exercises, you are removing elements of your emotional life that no longer serve your needs, and are replacing them with thoughts and feelings you want to have about yourself.

Let's take a minute to check in from last week:

- Did you get to do the meditation exercises every day?

- Were you able to create your own box, and store your worries and fears there temporarily?

- What did your box look like, and why did you choose that type of design?

- Did you have any emotional reaction to storing your worries like this?

- Did your worries cooperate with you when you did this practice?

- If not, what did they try to do or say?

- How did you cope with this, if it happened to you?

- After you stored your worries and fears, were you able to shift your meditation to a game of hide-and-seek, or another game?

- If so, what changes did you notice in your emotions after you did the meditation?

- What changes did you notice in your body after you did the meditation?

- Were you able to bring a sense of play into your daily life, "off the mat"?

- Were you able to release any memories that became conscious?

- Did you try the practice on becoming a camera, and snapping pictures of the memories as they arose in you?

- Did you try taking a real camera outside, to take some pictures?

- If so, what types of images were you drawn towards? Did they have a consistent theme, or were they very different from one another?

- When you wrote or spoke about your experience with your own memories, as well as the pictures you took, did you notice anything shifting emotionally?

- Did you sense any residual fear hanging around?

- Have your expectations of this program changed since last week? If so, how?

- Finally, how has instilling a sense of play changed the way you view storytelling, and your role in it?

Spend a few minutes recording the answers to these questions in your notebook or tape recorder. Settle yourself and take a moment to register how you're feeling right now. Is any particular emotion strong in you? If so, what does it feel like, and where is it located in your body? How does your body feel right now? Give yourself permission to feel whatever you're feeling, and ground yourself in that reality.

Impermanence

At the heart of every spiritual tradition is the concept of impermanence, that everything we see, everyone we know, every story we tell, has to end at some time. Most, if not all, spiritual traditions have rituals that deal with the transition between life and death. There are prayers, ceremonies, and places we go to visit the dead after they are gone. In the Chinese culture, there are days when graves are swept off and ancestors are worshipped. In Mexico, people celebrate the Day of the Dead, when families gather in cemeteries to remember their departed loved ones and children eat sugar skulls painted in garish colors.

But in many Western cultures, death is added to the list of things we fear. We avoid talking about it, or call it by other, less descriptive names. We say that someone has "passed away," or "gone to the other side." We shuffle our feet or look at the ground, anything to not have to look at our own mortality, or that of the people we love.

As we know from some of our previous exercises, fear is the enemy of storytelling. If there is a place we fear to talk about, chances are we will not "go there" storywise. We will shy away from the aspects of our stories that frighten us, so we will not get the benefits of telling it, personally, professionally, or otherwise. Readers of the story will sense that something is wrong, though they may not be able to put their finger on it. They will just know that they are being taken only part of the way to the destination.

The secret to deeper, richer characters is in accepting the idea of impermanence. Whether you choose to tell fictional stories, or those that come straight from your own life, holding the notion of endings in the back of your mind can help create strong connections with your intended audience. You may want to tell your stories at a meeting of likeminded individuals at a bookstore, or at your next family gathering. Connection with others depends on the universality of your message. And you can't get much more universal that the concept of impermanence.

It is not just our lives that have to come to an end. Impermanence extends to our homes and other possessions, our creations, and our relationships. It is sometimes daunting to be driven to create something, only to realize that our words, our paintings and other creations may not last forever. But there is also a softening that happens in our hearts when we realize that this is true. The words we choose to tell our stories become more carefully considered. The colors we choose for our paintings assume more brilliance. The images we frame in our photographs and film projects are packed with information we need to transmit to people that may come after us.

Impermanence, when viewed from this angle, becomes a goad, a rallying cry, a necessary evil, which can make our stories have an urgency that not only translates to the people we most want to reach, but transforms them, too.

What Makes a Story Universal?

If you've read any books on writing, chances are you

have heard the advice to tell universal stories, which speak to the greatest number of readers. You may have read books on story structure, or studied how to craft stories that can convince an agent to represent your work. Some of those books and classes have great merit, in that they can start you thinking towards making your work commercially viable. But to concentrate just on the universality of stories for commercial reasons robs them of their greatest potential before they're even out of the gate.

Stories are universal when they talk about experiences that people have, regardless of their experience. If a story is truly universal, it can translate as easily to a person in Thailand as to a person in Milwaukee. It has meaning for a rich person and a poor person, a Spanish person and an African person. This is easier said than done.

One way to think about telling universal stories, or to make your personal stories more universal, try thinking about experiences everyone has, no matter where they come from, no matter what language they speak. Death and impermanence, as we have seen, are two of them. Others may include the need to eat, sleep and breathe air, the need for family connections, the desire for love, and wanting to succeed and leave a mark on the world.

It's not just the subject matter, however, that makes a story universal. We all need to eat food, but telling someone a story about what you had for breakfast may or may not be interesting, depending on what happened, and how it is told. We must tell our stories authentically when we are first recording our experiences. But we must also look for ways to connect with our intended audience when we choose to share our stories with others.

Some people decide to do this by sharing their work in a writing workshop setting, and these certainly have their value. People who, like you, want to tell stories will listen as you read your story out loud, and then everyone takes turns commenting on the work in progress.

I have found that this is valuable only in as far as you are willing to take their suggestions, though. In general, writing workshops are not the most welcoming places. Most are there to tell their own stories, not to listen to the work of others. That fact, and repeated requests from some of my students, led me to write this book.

When people are first directed to telling stories, they may or may not have the confidence in their own abilities. As we have seen, many do not believe they have the right to tell their stories, or the tools to do so. Only by forming and maintaining supportive groups, with the sole intent of listening, can beginning storytellers truly flourish. It may be hard for others not to offer criticisms or helpful hints, but I have found that most storytellers lose confidence within the first few weeks, if this is done. The practice of reading stories out loud, if done regularly and in the practice of trusted friends or acquaintances, will hone almost anyone's "ear." We can all tell when someone we're talking to is tuning out, and this is a great tool to help adjust your stories so they are more universal in tone.

The Art of Listening

The secret, of course, lies in the art of listening. We may believe that we are great listeners, especially where our friends and family members are concerned. But when we are rushed, do we really listen to what our loved ones are saying?

Don't worry, it happens to all of us. We mean the best, but we have to cut off that phone call because we have a meeting in ten minutes, or we cancel dinner with one of our oldest friends because we simply can't fit it into our schedules. We may have gotten so caught up in our own stories, at least the mundane, everyday ones, that we can't seem to break our way out of them.

One very powerful tool we all have is the ability to listen. This may include the power to listen to our inner selves. Our meditations are one of the tools that help us get in touch with important feelings and bodily sensations.

But cultivating the ability and desire to listen to others is perhaps even more powerful as a tool of storytelling. Listening to someone else, completely, with your heart wide open, shows them that you truly care about them, as well as what they have to say. Adopting the posture of listening, with the body leaned forward, the eyes focused on the person speaking, and the head nodding slightly, conveys that you are a person who loves storytelling. You love people, and you love hearing about what they do. Welcoming stories into your life in this way cements the connection between you.

Meditation:

This week's meditation exercise will focus on impermanence, and the things we can't take with us, no matter how hard we may want to try. This will help us to wake up to our stories with a newfound urgency, and the desire for closure as well as communication. We do not have to lose someone in a literal way in order to contact this very motivating experience. Rather, we will work on contacting the feelings behind life's various endings, in order to use them in our stories.

Because this week's meditation and exercises involve death and other manifestations of impermanence, it's important to stay vigilant about your emotions. If you have lost someone close to you, especially if it has happened very recently, you may wish to skip this exercise for now, and move on to the next chapter, or just watch what comes up for you very closely. Know that if you are finding this new information too hard to handle, you can always seek the help of a qualified professional, your friends, or your family members.

This week, leave yourself a bit more time than usual so that you can feel grounded and supported again after your meditation sessions, and before engaging in any tasks you may find difficult, or which may involve lots of concentration. Confronting our sense of impermanence, perhaps for the first time, is not easy. Try to record your experiences truly and authentically, using your notebook or tape recorder. Give yourself some extra time, or some extra care, as you reach inside yourself for these new feelings and sensations.

In every great story, we have the sense that things may not always be this way, even though the story itself may not take us to that place. This can happen in great love stories, such as *Romeo and Juliet,* or inspiring dramas, such as *It's a Wonderful Life*. In either case, we know the characters will never be the same for having gone through the action of the story. Instead, the "ghosts" of the story, or how the characters used to be, will filter through our minds as readily as the new paths they have begun to tread. Exploring impermanence is what makes this possible.

- Find your way to your meditation place, leaving yourself enough time to move through the meditation session and post-meditation exercises. Make sure to close the door, and that you will not be disturbed for at least thirty minutes (forty-five if you have the time). Bring your notebook and a pen or pencil, or your tape recorder, if you are recording your experiences this way.

- Bring yourself into your meditation posture, taking a few minutes to make sure you're sitting upright, with dignity, whether you're seated in a chair, or crossed-legged on a cushion or pillows. Make sure your feet are flat on the floor if you're seated in a chair, and that you're not slouching. Resist the urge to lie down, because this only encourages spacing out or, more embarrassingly, falling asleep completely. Find that place of balance for your body.

- Now bring your attention to your breath as it moves into your body and then out again. Rather than trying to control your breath, or slow it down in any way, let your breath be what it is right now. Just observe it as it moves inside your body and is then expelled.

- Now bring your attention to the muscles of your body to make sure you are not holding tightness anywhere. If you are, just observe the feeling in your body, without trying to change it or pretend that it's not there. For each of the body parts you can relax, go ahead and do so, allowing each muscle to un wind at its own pace. Honor any part of your body that's not ready or willing to cooperate with your wishes just yet.

- Begin to notice the thoughts that move through your mind, taking the time to label them by saying "thinking" to yourself. Move into your Base Practice, labeling your thoughts and allowing them to leave your mind as you breathe out. Take five full breaths here, allowing your body and mind to relax.

- As you feel ready to do so, take a few minutes to connect your senses to your meditation practice, moving through each of them and labeling each in turn. Honor the five senses that bring you valuable information each second of each day, helping you to make your life's decisions.

- Once you have labeled your senses, come back to your Base Practice, taking five full breaths and labeling your thoughts as you notice them. Now bring to the front of your mind something or someone very dear to you. It may be a relative, a child, a friend or a teacher. Hold that person's face, or another detail, if you are working with an object or place, in your mind for a few seconds, allowing yourself to feel the emotions you associate with

148

this person. If you'd like, you can even take a few breaths to send this person, place or thing whatever you feel he, she or it needs, as we did in our lojong (also called tonglen) practice.

- As you hold this person, place or thing in your mind, also notice the sensations that are moving through your body. Where are these sensations concentrated, and what words would you use to describe them?

- Now allow this person, place or thing to dissolve in your mind, becoming ghostly and then disappearing completely. Imagine that this person, place or thing no longer exists in your life. Are there things you wish you had said before he, she or it disappeared? Are there things you wish you had done?

- Now notice the feelings you have in your body, and the thoughts that may be going through your mind. How are they the same or different from the thoughts you had before?

- Now visualize your own face in font of you, holding yourself in your mind for a few breaths. Breathe in your own pain, and breathe out, while sending yourself love, comfort and complete acceptance. As you are ready to do so, allow your own image to dissolve in front of you, imagining yourself becoming ghostly and then disappearing completely.

- Keep breathing, allowing yourself to register the changes in your thoughts and bodily sensations. Take five full breaths here. You are still here, and this is only an exercise.

- Think about what you would have wanted to say before you disappeared, and who you would have wanted to say it to. These are the rich details that will make your stories seem urgent and universal. Take a few breaths here, allowing your feelings and thoughts to completely percolate inside you.

- Now shift your perspective slightly. Rather than directing your meditation practice, as we have been doing so far, or allowing me to guide it for you, spend ten breaths just listening. Your mind may be freaking out at the thought of "dying." Or you may be terribly sad to think about losing someone dear to you. Or, you may feel completely free to think about existing outside a human body. Spend the entire time just listening to the myriad things your mind may be trying to tell you, without judgement.

- Allow your attention to return to your breath, and go back to your Base Practice. Label your thoughts as you notice them in your mind, and allow them to dissolve on the out breath.

- Notice any feelings you may be having now, as well as any changes in your body. Are there any areas where you are holding tension, or feel a sense of anticipation or dread?

- Take a moment to see if this meditation has released any memories in you. Did the image of dissolving activate anything in you? The fear of not existing? Without trying to control or analyze it, just observe these memories, as well as the corresponding feelings they release in your body.

- Return to your Base Practice, taking five full breaths and labeling your thoughts as you notice them in your mind. Allow your mind to return to its normal pace, releasing any leftover worries or fears that may have come up for you during this exercise. Let your mind clear and come out of the meditation.

Exercise:

Give yourself a few minutes to resume your normal consciousness when you come out of the meditation session. Getting in touch with impermanence is not something we tend to do on a daily basis, so the first time is generally hard for most people. Take some time to review your experiences in the meditation, and begin to record your experiences, using your notebook or tape recorder to do so.

Were you able to find a person, place or thing to work with the first part of the meditation? If so, who was this person, or what was the place or thing? Why is this person, place or thing so important to you? What did it feel like when this person began to vaporize and then disappear from your life? What sensations arose in your body as you thought about not having this person around anymore? Were you able to get in touch with what you might have wanted to say or do before that person was gone from your life?

When you shifted the meditation to holding your own image in mind, how did that feel? Were you able to do this easily, or was it embarrassing and strange? When you started to disappear from your own life, how did you react? What feelings came up for you, and what changes did you notice in your body? Did you have a sense of what you wanted more than anything to say before you left?

Did any fears come up for you, or were any old worries made stronger? Were you able to work with them enough to finish the meditation?

Were you able to spend at least ten breaths in and out just listening to the thoughts in your mind? How did it feel to allow yourself to do this? Did anything come up that was related to telling your personal stories, or sharing them with others?

Lastly, were any memories released for you? Sometimes, these can provide important clues as to what types of stories we really want to tell, or what stories are lurking just under the surface, waiting to be told. But if nothing came up for you this time, that's fine, too. You will have many opportunities to contact important memories for your storytelling purposes.

Record everything you can remember from your meditation session, using your notebook or tape recorder. Make sure to record the feelings that came up for you, any changes in your thought patterns, and the sensations you may have had in your body during the meditation. If any memories came up for you, try to record them as faithfully as you can, using smells, sights, sounds and textures to make the picture more three-dimensional. Remember to capture the feeling of being in your body at that moment in time.

When you are finished with the recording process, take a few minutes to just relax. Let yourself return to normal activities slowly, realizing that the work you've just done is particularly challenging, both for you personally and for your drive to wake up to your stories.

Check back in with your body. How are you feeling right now? Have any sensations shifted in your body, or do you notice any areas of tension or worry that may have accumulated? Are you experiencing any butterflies in your stomach?

As the week moves by, make sure to take part in this meditation exercise every day. You may choose to work with a different person, place or thing each time, or keep it the same, but it's important to remain with yourself as the second focus of the meditation exercise. You may find your feelings and bodily sensations shifting each time you do this, so please know that if anything becomes to extreme or uncomfortable, you can return to your Base Practice, or stop at any time. Losing ourselves can be a terrifying thing, or be a very liberating opportunity to make our conscious lives that much more meaningful. The choice is up to us.

Know that you are still conscious, still alive and capable of making changes to your life, through your personal efforts and behaviors, and through your ability to discover and share stories. Hold onto the sense of vitality within you, knowing that you have all the time you need to say and do the things you want to do.

Follow-Up:

Each day of this week, make sure to do the meditation practice on impermanence. In picturing a person, place or thing that is dear to you and then getting in touch with the feelings you have when it's gone will help to soften the heart, and to bring a sense of urgency to your storytelling. As you shift the meditation to get in touch with the same thoughts and feelings about your own time on the planet, bring your tolerance to what you might see or experience. What has been done or said in the past is not important. What matters is how you can move forward from this moment to bring greater awareness and authenticity to your daily life, to your meditation, and to your practice of storytelling.

Make sure to leave yourself plenty of time after each meditation session to record your thoughts and feelings, as well as any changes in your body. Then try to take these meditative experiences into your daily life. When we have a sense of impermanence, or endings, it's much harder to fly off the handle with people or get carried away by our emotions. It's not that we're stuffing them, or pretending they don't exist, they usually just don't have the chance to become as inflamed and out of hand while we're doing these practices.

Can you hold the sense of impermanence in your mind, while not getting overly sad about it? Can you use that sense of endings to bring a kind of sweetness to your daily activities? Does the deeper realization of your own mortality make your need to tell your personal stories any more poignant or more urgent?

Your challenge for this week is to carry the idea of impermanence and try to realize where you might be holding ghosts in your life. The person does not have to be dead in order to be a ghost in your life, just a person who left a lasting impression. Are you guided by voices that are not your own, to "stand up straight" or "smile and shake hands when you meet someone"? Is there someone's memory you're keeping alive, either consciously or unconsciously—an old lover, perhaps, or a professor you once admired in college? Has keeping this person's memory alive in your mind helped you, or has it stopped serving your purposes? Of course, there's no right answer, just the need to delve deeper into your own consciousness to discover what you need and what you don't.

Finally, take some time to develop your own personal art of listening this week. Invite someone to share their story with you, whether it's an exciting tale about a foreign trip this person just took, or a mundane night at home with the cat. Use inviting body language and encouraging interjections to help this person know you're interested. Most times, we're trained to think that no one cares about our experience. This week is about making that different.

Maybe you could try speaking with someone who really annoys you, to see how that feels. Being encouraging is also being active, so you assume a powerful position in the conversation even if you don't do much talking. It may be an experiment you don't want to repeat, but it will give you valuable insight into how far you're willing to go to tell your personal stories and listen to the stories of others.

If you'd like an additional challenge, choose one day of the week, when you might have a bit of extra time at the end of your meditation session. Sitting with your eyes closed, picture yourself as the character George in *It's a Wonderful Life*. You don't have to be white or male, just yourself, down on your luck. Imagine that something terrible has happened to you, and that you don't know how to make up for it. Maybe you are terribly broke, or you have caused an accident. An angel visits, and you find out that this is your personal guardian, who has always been with you, for your entire life (Feel free to name the angel, give it certain characteristics, clothing and gestures).

Look back at your time on this planet. Think about what might have happened if you were never here. What people wouldn't have met because of you? What would have happened to your parents? Your brothers and sisters? Your friends?

Let it sink in how you have affected the world by your presence. See how your simple (or not so simple) life has changed the lives of many, radiating outward. Notice how, even though you feel as if you have done bad things, or misguided things, you have also done wonderful things, which have touched many people. If you consider that we are all connected somehow, even if we have to invoke the old six degrees of separation rule, each of us has affected an enormous number of people, even if we're not receiving that kind of feedback on a daily basis.

If you have time to do this practice more than once during the week, that's great, but it's not necessary. Even doing this additional practice once in your life will give you a brand new perspective on where you stand in the world. Our time on this planet is short in the grand scope of things. But our potential impact, especially when carefully considered and authentically delivered, is truly great.

When you've finished visualizing how your close relationships and experiences would be different had you not been born, as well as the potential effects on the larger world, take a few minutes to write or speak about what you've seen. If you're having a particularly trying day, I find it's incredibly helpful to refer back to this notebook entry or section of tape. All of us have a unique role while we're here, and you are no different. Telling stories can help you realize this role.

Share what you've learned with others. You don't need to tell them about your meditations or exercises, unless you want to. But you can share the poignant quality we all access when we realize that life is indeed short. Open up to someone new today. Sharpen your senses and observational powers. Indulge your sense of play. Let yourself be truly vulnerable, and truly alive.

In the next chapter, we will get in touch with a sense of forgiveness, in order to let our own personal disappointments go, and replace them with the "story" we'd like to believe about ourselves. Forgiving what we haven't done or said leaves us wide open to change the script of our lives. By rewriting our lives from this point forward, we can take a healthy sense of confidence with us, while we start to change from the inside out. Knowing that we have a powerful tool like storytelling can make all the difference in getting us to take that first tentative step.

9 Waking Up to Your Stories

"[My stories] run up and bite me on the leg—I respond by writing down everything that goes on during the bite. When I finish, the idea lets go and runs off."

— Ray Bradbury

You don't have to be a lover of science fiction to love this quote by Ray Bradbury. When we are drawn towards storytelling, we may have no idea why. We may not know anyone who writes, or even reads that much. We just know that some sort of infectious bug has bitten us, and now we need to scratch the itch. This week, we'll do our final meditation and follow-up exercises before beginning to shape our experiences into stories next week.

For now, let's take a minute to check in:

- Did you do the meditation exercises on impermanence every day?

- Were you able to work with one person, place or thing, or a variety of people, places and things, calling their images to mind and then dissolving them?

- What happened in your mind when you "dissolved" this person, place or thing? Did any strong feelings come up for you and if so, what were they?

- Did you notice any changes in your body when you did this part of the meditation session?

- Were you able to get in touch with your own impermanence, by holding an image of yourself in mind, and then dissolving it?

- What did it feel like to watch your own image dissolve? Did any strong feelings come up for you, and if so, what were they?

- Did you notice any changes in your body when you did this second part of the meditation?

- Were any memories released for you during this meditation and, if so, what were they? Were you able to record them, with as many details as possible?

- Were you able to spend ten full breaths just listening to the thoughts and feelings that came up for you as a result of this meditation practice?

- Did you bring this practice into your daily life, allowing yourself to feel the poignancy of endings over which you have no control?

- Have you noticed any shift in your emotional life? For instance, is it as easy to lose your patience or get angry if you're holding the idea of impermanence in your mind?

- Have you noticed a greater urgency to tell your personal stories?

- Could you extend your practice by developing your own

personal art of listening in your daily life? Did you try it with a person you like, and with someone you don't really like very much?

- Did you try the additional challenge practice, of envisioning yourself as the main character of *It's a Wonderful Life* and imagining how the world would be different if you had not been born?

- If you tried this practice, what emotions came up for you? Did you notice any feelings or changes in your body?

- Did you take the time to write down your experiences from this additional practice?

- Finally, how have these practices changed the way you think about yourself and your storytelling work as you move forward?

As you are ready to begin work on this week's session, take a few minutes and record your answers to these questions, along with any other notes or observations you don't want to forget about your experiences last week. Then relax, put your notebook or tape recorder aside, and look inward. Are you experiencing any particular emotional patterns? Anything strong or distracting? Are you worried or scared? Delirious with joy? Bored out of your mind?

Check in with your body as well, locating the source of any strong emotions. Validate any pain or stiffness you may find in yourself. Let yourself be present and okay with whatever you find.

Letting Go of Disappointment

What I love about the Ray Bradbury quote that opens this chapter is that there is no sign of disappointment, no resonance of failure or regret. There is nothing but the present moment, no distractions, no wondering if it's good enough to be read by other people. Stories do not wait until you believe you are good enough. They simply exist, waiting to bite you on the leg.

As storytellers, our duty is to be brave enough to accept that bite. Bites, as we have begun to see, can hurt, literally and metaphorically. Realizing our mortality, or accepting that we are beings with constant fears and worries, may not correspond with the ideal version of ourselves, which we like to believe on a moment-to-moment basis. We may prefer to be thought of as brave and vigilant in the face of life's distractions, creative and handsome or gorgeous by turns.

By practicing our mediations, we get in touch with an array of life's feelings, from the pleasant to the unpleasant, and everything in between. We can take the "bite" of a story's arrival in our minds, and have the stamina to write down everything that happens during the bite. You may have already found that certain stories have begun to "dog" you, hanging around in the corners of your mind or invading your dreams at night. Your meditations, exercises, and follow-up activities may have spurred you to begin thinking of your characters, whether real or imagined, as "real" humans that will have qualities similar to people we know.

In addition to bringing ourselves into a brave space, where we are willing and able to be authentic with our feelings and welcoming of the ideas that come into our minds, we must also get in touch with things we regret. The places where we wish we could change something about our lives are the soft places, where the greatest concentration of human feeling and vulnerability can be found.

Being able to find these places is wonderful for convincing ourselves to go further with our stories. Though the Little Destroyers and the Underneath will still come up in all of us, to try to dissuade us from our goals, we can combat them with the tools we have learned. The more we can become comfortable with who we are right now, and also where we

160

have been, the easier it will be to overcome the fears and worries that lurk inside.

One key to conquering regret is to look at it, square in the face. This may seem simple to do, but you would be surprised at how clever we humans can be when we don't really want to look at something. If we've had a particularly embarrassing situation, or one in which we've failed miserably, we may tend to "rewrite" it in our minds, remembering ourselves as the victim of someone else's cruelty (that's a very popular one). We may recall ourselves being the brave or noble party, or tend to rescript the dialogue, particularly if we are engaged in retelling the story to someone else. Part of this may be to restore our lost dignity, but it comes at the expense of the truth.

Regret, if left unexamined, is one of the most pungent emotions, eating away at us like rust on a bicycle, or barnacles on the bottom of a boat. It may not look bad from the outside, at least not at first. But over time, regret can cause the entire structure of the story to fold in on itself, to die and disintegrate. It can leave us feeling better temporarily, but we never really forget the terrible feeling we've associated with that event. We've only buried it, under layers of subterfuge and lies. One way to rid ourselves of these terrible feelings is to examine them, and then to rewrite the situation, while awake and fully conscious. The first step towards making a transformation, in your life and in your stories, is to cultivate forgiveness.

Cultivating Forgiveness

Forgiveness is frequently misunderstood in our culture. Most religions have tenets that ask followers to "forgive and forget" or "turn the other cheek," and for the most part, these are great rules to live by. But forgiving while forgetting seems to involve brushing our real feelings aside, in order to "make nice," or re-establish balance between two people that may not agree. Likewise, turning the other cheek seems, at least from the outside, to endorse being beaten up. Are we supposed to let others continually hit us, all the while pretending that it doesn't hurt?

Non-violent conflict resolution definitely has its place in the world, and I doubt many of its proponents would advocate being beaten. This is, of course, a devil's advocate argument to illustrate a point. But why do we equate forgiveness with not having our own needs met? Why can't we forgive and have a sense of closure and satisfaction, that we have been heard and validated as well?

Admitting to embarrassing or painful moments in public has become so commonplace, it's almost a cliché. Some magazine interviewers will even ask some version of this question in celebrity-based articles, so we can have the feeling of knowing famous people better, or bringing them back down to our level. Like celebrities, we may even have our version of the "stock" answer, laughing uncomfortably at our disabilities and trying to get others in on the "joke." Some people may even use these stories to get laughs, sympathy, or attention.

But think about it for a minute—what has been the most painful moment in your life so far? Was it the loss of someone or something you thought was rightfully yours? The failure to live up to the mark you'd set for yourself? Assuming something and coming to find out you had the completely wrong idea about it? Whatever the details of your moment, chances are you're not in a hurry to repeat it, verbally or physically.

Admitting to embarrassment or failure is one very important quality of great stories. If we have to be perfect, so do our characters, and rarely are perfect characters interesting enough to read all the way through (with the possible exception of the child in *The Bad Seed*, who was perfect only on the outside.) Flaws make people interesting and unique, just as they infuse the characters in our stories with warmth, humor, pathos and adventure. As readers, we are barely able to tear our eyes away from the page when we encounter people like this.

Letting ourselves off the hook becomes part of this process. We're not striving for another way not to face what has become almost too painful to bear. Instead, we're trying to develop forgiveness for our role in our own foibles and failures, and then direct it towards the people we feel have hurt us. The point is not to "make nice," or pretend that everything is fine—far from it. True forgiveness takes us to a place where our authentic emotions have simply cooled, not ceased to exist. From this place of "cool boredom," as Buddhist teacher Chogyam Trungpa Rinpoche calls it, we are better able to face new challenges without flinching from them, all because we have become comfortable with what exists.

By adopting a broader definition of the word forgiveness, we make it possible for ourselves to practice it more effectively. By participating in new practices, which allow us to release the painful events of our past while not strengthening the negative thoughts we may have cultivated about them, we begin to break old, habitual patterns of covering over painful areas with half-truths. When that has been accomplished, we are freer, to tell the stories that were true, that we wish had been true, or that may well be true in the future sometime.

With forgiveness comes a new kind of freedom, to re-envision our lives as we wish they had happened. We are not trying to escape into a perfectly sterile and comfortable world, devoid of problems. We are constructing new stories we want to tell about ourselves, as one step towards becoming worthy of them. Rewriting the script is one way of using forgiveness to sculpt new goals in your life. And it provides a very important first step that makes taking that first step towards obtaining your goals that much easier.

Rewriting the Script

The act of waking up to our stories has many facets, as we have seen so far. But the moment we wake up to a story is the moment we decide to move forward, knowing what we know, regardless of where we may have come from. We may have grown up in utter poverty, with no opportunity for advancement and little encouragement. We may have lived through war, in refugee camps, not speaking the dominant language of our chosen countries. There may be abuse in our past, or supreme innocence and joy. But there are always stories that act like pieces of connective tissue to help facilitate our move into the future.

The first step towards rewriting the script is, of course, recognizing that life is like a script. We make plans, just as a screenwriter scripts out lines for actors to speak. We conduct ourselves in social groupings according to the traditional rules of our societies, we work and form relationships according to rules we have agreed upon. In this way, each of us scripts our own life, applying ourselves as school or not, working for a living or not, getting married and having children or not. Each of these choices, along with myriad others, is reminiscent of the choices a screenwriter must make in writing a movie or television show. What should happen to the main character this week? And what will the results of his or her choices manifest in future episodes?

We make these choices every minute of every day. From the mundane, such as what to have for lunch, to the more daring, such as whether or not to attend training to be a flight attendant, our minds create stories that influence our behaviors. If we're having a bad day, and the application for flight attendant school is due, we may tell ourselves, "I don't know why I'm thinking about doing this. It's so stupid, and I'll have to wear that uniform. Plus, I'm probably not smart enough to get in."

Yesterday, you may have been over the moon about the opportunity for a steady job with benefits and the ability to travel all over the world. Today, the story has shifted, and your inner voices have convinced you not to take an important action. The urge for change has not shifted, however. When your bad mood has passed, you will find yourself restless again. It may come out in spending too much money, or eating too much, or becoming jealous when someone at work shows you their vacation photos.

As human beings, we are programmed to think first and act later, unless we're under direct attack. Sometimes, having a built-in deterrent is a great thing, providing us with the distance we need to make an informed decision. For example, it probably came in handy when you wanted to go skydiving with the flu. But other times, we may have to develop a mechanism that overrides this tendency to act later. Examples might include places we're afraid to go, but will almost certainly enrich our experience, such as going back to school, trying a new career path, or dipping our little toe back into the dating pool two years after a bad breakup.

Rewriting the script can help us to achieve this override, and even convince our think-first-act-later mechanism to go along willingly with our plans. Once we have admitted and understood that life is like a movie script, we can begin to look at the way we've scripted our own lives. Are there any places you won't let yourself go, even though you are attracted to them? Some examples might include wanting to play a new sport, but being afraid that you will look silly, or seeing a commercial for a jewelry-making class on television, but being afraid that this line of work might not make you enough money as your "real" job. You may even think about writing a book of your personal stories, but not want to tell anyone, lest you get no support or encouragement from your friends and family members.

These are all examples of how we script our lives, or let

others script them for us. We put ourselves into little boxes, such as, "I'm a liberal," or "I'm a Christian," or "I'm a sports guy," or "I'm not a jeans girl." This helps us to develop a concrete sense of self. We're comfortable this way, because we recognize ourselves when we are confronted with the minute-by-minute decisions we have to make. Though there is nothing inherently wrong with this, it does tend to limit our experience of the world.

As we recognize the script we have all "written" for our lives, we can also begin to think about ways in which we may want to make changes. Perhaps we are just sick of our job, and want to do something different with our time. Maybe we want the ability to do more volunteer or church work. Or perhaps we simply want to have more fulfilling relationships with others. I believe we can all make these desired changes, if we are willing to do the work to break old, negative patterns of belief about ourselves and our abilities. But that is easier said than done.

Rewriting the script of our lives takes the courage to look deeper within ourselves, and the tenacity to keep trying, no matter what you see there. You may find things about yourself that you'd prefer not to admit. You may see things you wish hadn't happened. But if you keep working with these "scripts," you will find that you are making daily progress towards your goals.

Meditation:

This week, our meditation exercise will focus on forgiveness, and using it to break patterns of inaction in our lives. We will start by letting go of disappointment, and begin to realize that forgiveness is possible, no matter how dark our past may be. Once we have begun to get in touch with forgiveness, we can use it to address old, painful areas in ourselves, and in our interactions with other people.

Since we'll be delving even deeper into the past, and examining events that may not be pleasant, I want to remind you to be careful about your emotions. Please move slowly and deliberately through the meditation and subsequent exercises, being vigilant towards the feelings that come up for you, and how they make you feel in your body. Always know that you can stop doing the exercise if something becomes too painful for you, and skip forward, or come back to it later. And as always, if you find that you need to speak to a professional about your feelings, please don't hesitate to do so.

As you move through this week's exercises, don't be shy about giving yourself some real credit. You've made it almost all of the way through this program of waking up to your stories, and you're doing very brave and important work for yourself. If you have not already begun to see the kind of results you had hoped for, I believe you will start to see them after this week.

Make sure to record the experiences in your meditation and post-meditation exercises using your notebook or tape recorder. Some of you may find your way to forgiveness easily, and be able to move past the blocks that disappointment sometimes sets in our way. Others may find this a harder exercise, and may need more time to develop forgiveness for themselves and others. There is no right amount of time to spend on this. All that's required is the true desire to see change, in ourselves, and in the stories we tell about these experiences.

- Come into your meditation space, making sure you will have enough time to do the meditation session and record your experiences in the post-meditation. Close the door, and make sure you will not be bothered for at least thirty minutes. Make sure you have your notebook and a pen or pencil, or your tape recorder, if you are recording your experiences in this way.

- Come into your meditation posture, giving yourself a few minutes to balance yourself. Make sure you're seated upright, whether you're seated on the floor, on a cushion or pillows, or in a chair. If you're seated in a chair, place your feet flat on the floor to establish more of a connection with the earth. Feel yourself pulled upward by an invisible string at the top of your head. Try not to over arch your back, or slouch too much. Don't lie down, either, so you remain as awake as possible. Adjust yourself until you find your perfect balance.

- Begin to notice your breath as it moves in and out of your body. Don't try to set a pace with your breath, but just watch what it's doing right now. Take five full breaths here, just observing.

- Look into the sensations of your body, shifting your awareness slightly. Are you holding tightness anywhere? Do you feel relaxed, or sick to your stomach? Irritated and annoyed? Whatever you find in your body, let it be. Some of your muscles will probably relax as you bring your attention to them. The rest are fine the way they are now.

- Now start to notice the thoughts that move through your mind. As you notice them, touch them lightly and say, "thinking," to yourself. Take a few minutes to establish your Base Practice, just letting your thoughts arise as they will and then releasing them on the out breath. Take five full breaths here, labeling your thoughts and letting them go.

- Now take a moment to connect each of your senses to your mediation practice. One by one, move through each of your senses, labeling it with, "seeing," "hearing," "touching," tasting," and "smelling." Notice how each sense seems to intensify as you bring your attention to the service it provides for you.

- After you have labeled each of the senses, return to your

168

Base Practice. Take five full breaths here, labeling your thoughts when they come into your conscious mind.

- Take a moment to bring forward an event from your past. It may already be very present for you, or it may require some prompting. But it should be a situation that brought embarrassment or pain of some kind. We don't have to visualize the most painful thing ever. It could just be saying something by mistake to the postal clerk this morning, or failing to remember your anniversary. It may be something you did yourself, or something someone did to you.

- When you have this situation visualized in your mind, just hold it there for a few minutes, letting your feelings come to the surface. Recognize your feelings, and honor them. Allow them to be what they are. Now begin to notice them in your body. How have the feelings in your body changed since you began to hold this visual image in your mind? Have they stayed the same?

- When this painful situation has played out in your mind, stop the frame, as if you were a movie projector. Just do it suddenly, without thinking about what you might find. When you've frozen the image there, what do you see? Is it an image of you, and if so, what expression do you have on your face? What are you doing in the image? Is someone else there with you and if, so, what is that person doing or saying?

- Feel the emotions moving through you now. If it is disappointment, label it, silently, to yourself. If it is anger or sadness or fear, take a moment to label it. If it is something else entirely, take a moment to label it as well.

- Now rewind the film in your mind. We've all seen images of film or television shows rewinding, so try to bring that into your mind now. When you get back to the beginning of the situation you envisioned, pause the image, as if on a VCR or DVD player.

- Spend a few minutes thinking about what you would have preferred to have happened. Did you want someone to notice you, or show you love? Do you wish you hadn't said something, and instead said something different? Just let your mind spin out a new scenario, which is very much like this one except for one crucial difference—the outcome.

- When you have your new scenario in mind, let the pause button go and let your movie play out in the new way you'd preferred to have it happen. If you wish you had said something different to someone, watch yourself say the exact right thing. If you wish someone had not done something painful to you, see yourself moving through that situation without pain. Or, if you'd prefer, tell that person that he or she hurt you, and allow them to apologize. Allow this new scenario to play out in its entirety.

- When your movie has come to a stop, let the screen go dark. Check in with yourself, to see what feelings you're having right now. Look in your body, to see what sensations are concentrated there. How has this painful or disappointing situation made you feel, and how does seeing it play out differently affect you? Are you beginning to see how you have the power to determine how life's events shape you?

- Take five full breaths here. Now bring the same situation up again, in its original version, and hold it in your mind. If you are working on something you wish you hadn't said or done, picture your own face. If you are working with someone who may have hurt you in the past, picture that person's face. You have already rewritten the past, in a way, and may have perhaps told the other person that he or she hurt you, and allowed them to apologize. Now, using one or the other image in your mind, start to send whatever you feel that person needs, using the techniques we used in tonglen meditation. If it's you, perhaps you want to send comfort, or tissues, if you're crying. If it's someone else, you may to send a hug, so that person isn't frightened or angry enough to hurt someone else. You could send a warm blanket, or an hour of time with nothing to do—whatever you feel inspired to extend to that person.

- When you have done that, freeze the frame again. Silently, to yourself, say, "I forgive you," to the person you're holding in your mind. Notice how it feels to say those words "aloud" in your mind. Do you feel powerful? Ashamed? Tolerant? Or another emotion?

- Bring your awareness to your body, and see how the feelings in your body might have changed since you began this meditation. Has anything changed since you were able to extend your forgiveness to yourself or another person? If so, how has it changed?

- Now bring your attention back to your breath, returning to your Base Practice by labeling your thoughts as you notice them in your mind. As you notice each thought, let it dissolve as you release it on the out breath. Take five full breaths here, allowing yourself to turn inward.

- Allow your mind to return to its normal rhythms, while letting go of any residual worries, fears or other emotions that may be plaguing you. Let go of any feelings that may have concentrated in your body, as your mind clears and you come out of the meditation.

Exercise:

When you are finished with your meditation session, take a few moments to come back to your regular consciousness. When we visualize painful or embarrassing moments, part of us is bound to feel that level of pain or embarrassment all over again, so take it easy for a few minutes.

When you feel ready, record the experiences you had while in the meditation session. Write down the feelings, sensations and other details, using your notebook or tape recorder.

Were you able to visualize a painful or embarrassing situation you had been through? If so, was it in the recent past, or the distant past? What were some of the details of this situation? Were any other people there and, if so, who were they? Did your pain come from something you wish you had done or said, or from something someone else did or said to you?

Was it extremely painful, or just slightly so? Take a few minutes to describe the feelings that came up in you when you saw this experience again in your mind. Remember to also describe the physical sensations your body may have been going through as well.

Were you able to freeze the last frame as this situation ended in your mind, as if you were a movie projector? If so, what was the last image you saw as it was frozen? Were you in it? If so, what did you look like and what were you feeling?

Were you able to rewind the movie in your mind? Did you spend a few moments thinking about the way you would have preferred that things happen? If so, take a few moments here to describe how you wanted this scenario to unfold. If you can, add details such as facial expressions and lines of dialogue, if you had specific words in mind for yourself or another person to say.

Afterwards, were you able to play back this new version of the scenario, with your rewritten ending? If you were working with another person, did you tell that person that he or she hurt you, and allow them to apologize for their role in that?

Were you able to send that person, whether it was yourself

or someone else, whatever you felt they needed at that moment? Was it easy or hard to do this? Were you able to hold that person's face in mind, and then say, "I forgive you?" If so, did you believe it when you said that, or did you still feel hurt or angry towards this person?

What feelings came up for you when you forgave him or her? Were you relieved? Still angry and hurt? Or something else?

What sensations came up in your body when you forgave this person? Did you feel tighter or looser? Tired, or filled with energy?

Lastly, were any memories released as a result of this practice? Did you see yourself in any similar situations as a result of visualizing this particular scene? If so, please take a moment to describe in as much detail as you can the memory you contacted. If not, that's fine, too. Just move on to the next step.

Record everything you can remember from your meditation session, using your notebook or tape recorder. Record your feelings and any changes that might have occurred in your body as well. Use descriptive words that give clues about smells, tastes, sounds, images and textures, if they came up. You want to be able to transport yourself back to this moment when you refer to your notes in the future.

When you finish recording your memories, feelings and bodily sensations, sit for a few minutes with your feelings at this moment. Allow your mind to return to its normal concerns. Give your body a quick check to see if any further shifts have occurred.

Do this meditation exercise each day this week. Leaving yourself about thirty minutes for the guided portion of the meditation, and then the recording portion afterwards. You may want to work with the same hurtful or embarrassing situation, or choose to work with a new one each time, whichever seems most helpful to you. If something becomes overwhelming, please return to your Base Practice, labeling your thoughts when you notice them in your mind.

The work you're doing is extremely valuable, both in your daily life and as it relates to waking up to the stories inside you. Your ability to move beyond disappointment, by forgiving yourself and others, paves the way for new action. Cultivate that part of you that wants to move forward, despite all odds. Know that your stories are one valuable part of that path towards fulfillment.

Follow-Up:

For each day of the new week, carve out some time for yourself to do the meditation exercise on moving past disappointment and cultivating forgiveness. After some time spent softening the heart by getting in touch with impermanence last week, we're now strengthening our resolve and preparing ourselves for the action of writing (or recording, if you're using a tape recorder). As we see that we are not just products of what has already happened, we begin to realize that the world is a wide-open place, crammed full of possibility.

Leave plenty of time for recording your experiences. Then, as with last week's exercise, try to take these experiences into your daily life as a new kind of practice. If we have given ourselves the freedom to cast off disappointment, we may find ourselves more easily granting forgiveness to others. So this week, if someone hurts you, or acts in a self-involved manner, try sending that person whatever you think he or she needs. It's very easy to get caught up in the emotions of the moment, so if that happens to you, it's completely fine. Just have the intention to try a different way when this type of moment arises again.

If you are someone who's very hard on yourself, and have been trying to forgive something you've said or done in the past (or haven't done or said), trying catching yourself in the act of criticizing yourself. If the voices of the Little Destroyers come up, try to immediately flip the dialogue. Send yourself whatever you feel you need at the moment—a raise, some chocolate, a road trip—and move into forgiveness.

Be vigilant about your emotional shifts. Can you get beyond any disappointments that may be strong in your life? Are you able to say, "I forgive you" in your mind and really mean it? And how does it feel to be able to form that bridge between stagnation and action in your mind?

This week's off the mat challenge is to look for areas you tend to get stuck in the past, or in beliefs that keep you grounded in the past. Do you consider yourself an optimist? A Republican? A redhead? A Lithuanian? Are these beliefs integral to who you are? If they shifted, would you be another person entirely?

If you find yourself harboring beliefs that seem to keep you from trying new things, or experiencing new ideas, try working with these in your meditation practice. How would it feel to be a Democrat, a blond, or a Korean? Only you will know the difference between beliefs that bolster your life and those that keep you from enjoying it. Allow yourself to entertain all of the options, without fear that your core self will somehow be eroded in the process.

When you have gathered five days' worth of this information, spend the next two days waking up to your first story. Using your notebook or your tape recorder, record the ways in which you want to move forward in your life. Rather than making it a list of goals, try telling it like a story. For example, you might start out by writing, "I started working at this job about two months ago, and at first, I thought it was going to be fun. But now, I'm going to ..."

Write or speak it in the present tense as much as possible, using phrases such as, "I'm going to ..." or "Now, I'm ..." or even "I've started to ..." This keeps you thinking about rewriting the script of your life, or at least the chunk of it that lies immediately ahead. By keeping your mind focused on the near future, it doesn't get too overwhelming, and also it gives you the sense that not only can you reach these goals, you're already doing it.

Have fun with it, and use as many details as you can:

- What do you look like in this story?
- How are you dressed?
- How do people refer to you?
- Who are your friends?
- How do they treat you?
- Do you work?
- If so, what is your position?
- If not, how do you spend your time?
- Do you have a lover or mate?
- If so, what is this person like?
- How do you spend your time with your lover or mate?
- What are your relationships with your family members like?
- Do you have children?
- If so, what are your children like?
- Do they have hobbies? Do they like school?
- What is a typical day like for you?

- How do you spend your mental energy?

- What are your goals or aspirations?

- What is your spiritual life like?

- What does your body look like?

- How does your body feel?

- How is your emotional life?

- Are you continuing to meditate?

You are free to use these questions as prompts, or use some of your own devising. Go wild, and feel free to write whatever comes to mind. Remember that no one else will read or hear this story unless you choose to share it with them, so there is nothing you could possibly do that would be wrong. Let your imagination be your guide, showing you where you may really want to be, even if you may not want to admit that to yourself.

When you are finished, take a moment to read over or listen to what you've just recorded. Some of you may feel embarrassed by the grandeur of your dreams, but make yourself sit still, not judging yourself or the story, until you have read or heard it in its entirety. If you find yourself getting emotional or tensing up, remember to breathe and let your thoughts leave you on the your breath. Honor what you have been brave enough to tell yourself. Let that stand as a testament to what you can achieve, if you set your mind to it.

For an additional challenge this week, I'll give you a choice:

The first choice is to find one other person to tell about your story. It may be someone close to you, if that's what you're comfortable with, or it may be a complete stranger, or someone you know only from an Internet chat room. Watch how this makes you feel emotionally. Are you scared? Proud?

Ebullient? Make sure to notice any shifts in your body as well when you tell someone else about your story. (Note: you don't have to tell them the whole story, if you don't want to, just that you have written it. Of course, if you choose to read your story to someone, that's great, too.)

The second choice is to take one action that brings you closer to achieving the life you wrote or spoke about in your story. That may mean that you dedicate yourself to getting a better job, by updating your resume and posting it online, or making more friends, by joining a club or association of some kind. You may wish to find a partner, and take the action of signing up with an Internet dating service, or want to establish storytelling as an integral part of your life, by vowing to write or speak your personal stories at least three times per week.

No matter which one you choose, take the time to truly connect with what you're doing. Don't just do it to fulfill a "requirement." Instead, recall your experience with impermanence last week. Vow to make your actions intentional and meaningful.

Just as you got in touch with how the world would have been changed without your presence, look inside and see what other goals might need attending to. They may be practical goals, like losing weight or getting more sleep, but they may also be more esoteric in nature. Listen carefully. Your mind may be trying to tell you that it wants to try painting, or ice skating, or scrapbooking.

If you work this practice in once per week, that's great. Some people prefer to achieve one goal, then set another. And others like to give themselves new to-do lists whenever the seasons change. Remember that this is not about racking up brownie points, or waiting to receive a reward for our work. Rather, it's about exploring the deepest parts of ourselves, and making room, by moving beyond disappointment and cultivating forgiveness, to try potentially life-altering things.

Always make sure to check in with your emotions when you're doing this practice, as well as anything that might be going on in your body. Record how telling another person about your story made you feel or, if you chose the second option, how taking one action towards achieving the life you wrote about in your story felt to you. Go into as much detail as you can, going past what you formerly thought of yourself to discover entirely new "yous" living inside.

If you decide to, try to share your story with others in more personal ways. You may choose to do these exercises with another person, and share the stories when you're finished. Bearing witness to another person's shame, disappointment, and forgiveness can sometimes be very empowering for both people. And being part of another person's dreams can also be pretty exciting as well!

If you're not comfortable with that now, don't worry about it. You will know if and when you want to share your stories. For now, know that you have achieved something very rare. You have authentically plumbed the depths of yourself, and come out with a very real story about where you want to go from here.

In the next chapter, we'll talk about what it means to finally write down or record your stories, and to get in touch with the feeling of accomplishment that comes with telling others about our experiences. We will begin to bring together all of the meditations and exercises we've done so far, coming to the best and most personalized way to work for you.

Together, we are forming a human record, connecting ourselves to people and places we may not know. We are linking ourselves to history, and forming a path for future generations to follow. Making time for stories in our lives can help us to move beyond the past, establish new ground rules for the present, and move into the future with our arms wide open.

10 Writing it Down

"The one who tells the stories rules the world."

— Hopi Indian proverb

We've made quite a journey so far, in waking up to our stories, and we are almost at its end. It doesn't matter if your goal is to rule the world or just have your fair shake at defining history. Our stories are still as important as those of famous people, world leaders, and even great artists and inventors.

This week, we'll change the usual format in order to begin the process of forming your personal narratives into stories.

But first, let's take a moment to check in from last week:

- Were you able to do your meditation exercises every day of the week?

- Were you able to move beyond the disappointing, hurtful or embarrassing moment you chose to work with?

- Was another person involved, or were you working with yourself?

- When you played out this painful scenario in your mind, what feelings came up? Were you able to label the feeling?

- Were you able to freeze-frame your mental movie on its last frame?

- If so, what was the image like? How did it make you feel?

- Were you able to think about how you wanted the scene to unfold, and then rewind your mental movie to make that happen?

- If so, what feelings came up for you?

- What changes did you notice in your body?

- Were you able to hold the image of the person who hurt you, whether it was yourself or someone else, and send that person whatever you felt he or she needed, using tonglen meditation?

- If you were working with another person, were you able to say, "I forgive you," and explain how that person hurt you?

- If so, did you really mean it, or were you practicing for now?

- Were you able to allow your mental movie to go dark, and to return to your Base Practice?

- Was your mind still active, or was it still when you did this?

- Lastly, were any memories released for you as a result of your practice this week? If so, were you able to record them in detail?

Now let's think about the exercise and follow-up:

- Were you able to work with the same or different people in your meditation sessions, for the first five days of the week?

- Did you move your practice off the mat, bringing it into your daily life?

- Did you start to notice areas where your beliefs about yourself had held you back from trying new adventures?

- Could you more easily identify the disappointments in your life?

- Did you find yourself cultivating forgiveness, for yourself and others?

- Were you able to see your way clear to taking action, now that some of the obstacles of disappointment had been removed?

- Did you record any changes to your feelings and bodily sensations?

- Were you able to spend the last two days of the week writing the story of how you want your life to be, or one portion of your life?

- If so, what were some of the most important details of your story?

- Did you read your story over to yourself? If so, how did that make you feel?

- Did you choose to share your story with another person? If so, what feelings came up?

- Did you choose to take one new action to bring about the life you wrote or spoke about in your story?

- And finally, were you able to recognize any other version of you that might have been living inside all this time? What does this version of you want, and how can you help it go about living its dreams?

Before you start on this week's exercises, take a few moments to write down or speak the answers to these questions, along with any other feelings you may be having about last week's work, and/or moving forward with your stories. When you have finished, look inside. Are any emotions particularly strong in you now? How is your body feeling? Let your mind and your body know that you are here to nurture them. Bring your awareness to your complete self, and the stories sleeping inside you.

Creative Venting

So far, the techniques we've used to wake up to our stories involve looking within to discover the kinds of stories you may be drawn towards telling, and then recording all of your images, feelings, and bodily sensations. In effect, we're using a kind of creative venting to get started.

The reason this is a perfect way to begin is because we all do this, every day. We complain to co-workers about something our boss has done, tell our lover about our childhood, or call our families to give them a run-down of our recent activities. Stories are organic to the way we live our lives and, because of that, our existence is given more meaning in the telling of them.

Some people may have a problem with the word vent, as it implies a sort of dumping of one's uncontrolled emotions onto another person. But that's not what we're doing here. Careful internal work is combined with creative venting to ensure that nothing is held back, and that all thoughts, feelings, random fragments and dangling participles are recorded for future use.

Right now, we're not worried about publishing our stories, so it's fine to vent. Much like we use diaries to "listen" to us, recording feelings and experiences for use in storytelling is cathartic and healing. No one will read this version of our work, if we don't want them to, so there is no risk of hurting anyone.

If you decide to publish your stories in the future, and they feature someone you know and have trouble with, or even if this person is readily recognizable by their features, qualities, or words, you may wish to change the person's name. Of course, part of this is to alleviate hurt feelings or possible recriminations (they may be reading this book, too!), but it can also fend off potential defamation lawsuits, depending on how harsh (or true) the story is.

Venting does not have to have a negative connotation, as long as we're clear about why we want to tell our stories, as well as our role in them. At this point, our role is to write or speak our stories, with the knowledge that if we decide to make them public in the future, we have tools to alleviate any trouble that might arise.

The Role of Memory

As we begin to write our stories down, or speak them into tape recorders, it's also important to consider the role of memory. We have already touched on this briefly in Chapter 4, when discussing recent publishing scandals involving James Frey, JT Leroy and Nasdijj. But we do ourselves a disservice, as storytellers, to worry about the role of memory at this stage. It is, of course, wrong to misrepresent oneself and one's work as being true when it's fiction, especially when it's done simply to get into print. But again, this is something that is malleable, and can be worked with, within reason.

The role of memory is always subjective. You see the world through your eyes, and I see it through mine, with all the inherent issues, cultural prejudices, and needs that each of us has. Unless there is a written record, such as a report card, an arrest record, or a published news story, the details will always be dependent on how a particular person saw something happen. The Japanese movie *Rashomon* shows this perfectly as four people, each of whom has seen a terrible rape and murder, tell four completely different stories about the incident.

The point is that there is no right or wrong when you're starting out. Everything becomes colored by memory as soon as it's filtered through our minds and our experiences. It's not important to be historically accurate, as long as you are honest about the feelings that came about as a result of this experience. If you've decided to publish your stories, again, it's critical to be honest about how you represent the type of work you're doing. But there is another factor that becomes almost more significant to your storytelling, and that is intention.

Intention

For every story you begin to craft from your notes, your meditations and your experiences, ask yourself: why do I want to tell this story? Am I angry? Do I want revenge? Am I trying to get attention and love from a wider audience?

Pinpointing intention is important in telling personal stories because, at times, the details we have observed can overlap with the objective we want to serve. Privately, we may want to be seen or heard, or to be part of fashioning our culture. But publicly, we may be driven to toe a politically correct line, or some other limiting philosophy.

It's always best to ask ourselves these questions before we write down our stories, not in order to limit our powers of expression, but to focus on achieving exactly what we're after. Are we prone to making ourselves better by inventing certain details? Are we braver and more pious in our stories than we are in real life? Or do we want to invoke sympathy by seeming worse off and more pathetic than we really are?

This is not to say that your stories already suffer from this malady. Rather, it's something to bear in mind as you begin to take your stories out of your minds and notes and make them live on paper, or as molecules of sound.

Truth

Whether we're fashioning a fiction or non-fiction story, truth is always subjective. Though it's our duty to strive to recreate incidents as faithfully as we can, there will be at least one person who says to you, "It didn't happen that way!"

Learning to hear this person, and yet still believe in your own faculties of recollection, is an important part of this journey. If our stories are treated with respect and honesty, they will bring us authenticity and happiness in return. But sometimes, striking this balance can feel like a wrestling match run amok in your mind.

My suggestion is this: if a memory seems particularly strong, yet potentially damaging, let it sit for a few days before touching it again, either with your meditation practice or in your act of recording it. After some time has passed, try to get in touch with it again. Does it still have the same power? Or has your remembrance of this moment changed?

Neither choice is inherently bad. Finding the balance between questioning ourselves, in order to find the most authentic way of touching a memory, and censoring ourselves, is what we're after. Balance feels like a good conversation you have with a friend. There are no harsh words exchanged, and no judgement, no matter how silly you act. There is only good-natured consideration of one another's viewpoints.

On the other hand, judgement feels threatening, or as if a giant thumb is pressing down on us. There's no room to have our voice heard. We may feel as if the other person's viewpoint (or, in this case, the other person's perceived viewpoint) blocks out all the light, or becomes the entire picture. If you're having an experience like this second example, your story may really be worth telling, simply because your voice has become so stifled about it.

The point is that the inner voice of doubt or condescension cannot exist without you, same as the Little Destroyers and the Underneath. If you need to, try to talk to this voice. Tell it that you will be careful about hurting others if it will allow you to work in peace. You may even want to promise you will tell its story, as long as it promises to cooperate with you.

Writing It Down

So far, we have done nine meditation sessions, with exercises and follow-up activities. Below are the names of the chapters, along with a list of sub-heads for each one. Using your notebook or tape recorder, review the notes you made during all of your meditation sessions, exercises, and follow-up activities.

Then review the list below:

Our Silence – Silence and Complicity

Our Need for Stories:

- An Explanation of the World Around Us
- A Way to Honor the Supernatural
- A Way to Entertain Ourselves
- A Way to Gain Immortality, by Connecting with Our Ancestors
- A Way to Express the Beauty of Human Existence

The Uses of Stories:

- Healing from Abuse and Neglect
- Connecting With Relatives and Family Members

- To Leave Something Behind
- To Express Ourselves and the World We Live In
- To Become More Visible
- To Ensure That Our Way of Life Continues

What Stands in the Way:
- Lack of Time
- We Don't Feel Qualified to Write
- Other People Tell Stories Better Than We Do
- Shyness
- We Don't Have the Right to Tell Our Stories
- We Might Hurt Someone
- Maybe it Didn't Happen as I Remember It
- It's Only Good if I'm Going to Publish It

Taming Our Fears:
- Receiving Our Stories
- Fear, and the Fear of Fear Itself
- Boundaries
- Fearing Our Own Nature
- Welcoming Fear

Awakening Love:
- (What's So Funny 'Bout) Peace, Love and Understanding?
- Peace
- Love
- Understanding

188

Getting Out of the Way:

- Thought into Action
- The Last Vestiges of Fear
- A Sense of Play
- Living Outside Time

Ghosts:

- Impermanence
- What Makes a Story Universal?
- The Art of Listening

Waking Up to Your Stories:

- Letting Go of Disappointment
- Cultivating Forgiveness
- Rewriting the Script

For each chapter, choose one item from the list, Chinese-menu style. If the chapter name does not have any choices underneath, write down or speak your reason or motivation for that chapter. For instance, for Our Silence, which has no choices underneath, you might record how you are silent, or why you are silent about your personal stories. Please also record how you want to change this.

Go down the list, picking the choices that seem most prevalent for you. At the end of the exercise, your list might look something like this:

I am silent because I never realized anyone would care about my stories.

I want to change this by sharing my stories with others.

A Way to Express the Beauty of Human Existence

Healing from Abuse and Neglect

Lack of Time

Fearing Our Own Nature

Love

A Sense of Play

The Art of Listening

Letting Go of Disappointment

What you've just done is write out a very brief outline of a story, the story you woke up to while reading this book and doing its exercises. Can you see how this story might progress, depending on who's writing it? There is a person or character that's silent and doesn't realize she can speak up. She vows to change this by sharing her stories with others. She is drawn to expressing the beauty of human existence, and wants to heal from abuse and neglect. Though she has a lack of time (a built-in conflict), and a fear of her own nature as an abused person, she cultivates love, a sense of play, and the art of listening in order to let go of disappointment. Drop the curtain.

Now, using the choices you have written or spoken on your list, tell your story. Think about it for a few minutes before writing in your notebook or speaking into your tape recorder. Remember to think about your intention before you begin. Are you trying to do one thing and hoping for something else? An example might be trying to seem interesting while secretly hoping people will applaud. Cement your intention in your mind before beginning.

Try to set future goals aside for now, and just focus on the joy of telling your unique story. Why are you silent? Has your silence made you complicit in not helping to shape your culture? And how do you want to change this? You may choose to not change it, but peacefully co-exist with it. Remember, this is your story.

Now, what is your primary need for stories in your life? Do you want to change the world, by reflecting and explaining society as a faceless place that does not nurture its citizens? Or are you drawn towards the supernatural, and finding a way to bond with it? Ancient storytellers often wove rain or thunder gods and goddesses into their tales, or made them as ancestors. Look into why you need to tell stories. Spend a few minutes really thinking about it before starting on this part of your story.

Now let's look at how you will use stories in your life. Of course, you can choose more than one use, but let's focus on one now, for this story. Pick the one that jumps out at you, without thinking about it too much. Do you want to connect more with your children, grandchildren, relatives or other family members? Or simply express yourself, after spending too much time in silence? Or maybe you want to become more visible, especially if you have come from a culture that doesn't value who you are or what you do. Spend a few minutes writing or talking about the ways you can think of to use stories in your life. You may even find some that are not on this list, since it's not meant to be complete, just suggestive. Let your imagination really crank up here, as you begin to visualize all the ways you can use your stories in your life.

Move on to the next section, to the things that tend to stand in our way. What stands in the way of your telling your stories? Do you lack the time or space in your life to devote to something that does not pay the bills (yet)? Do you believe that others are better storytellers than you are? Or perhaps you are worried that if you tell your stories, or share them with other people, someone will get hurt. Sometimes, this happens when we tell the truth. But remember, no one will read or hear your stories unless you decide to share them, so try to be as honest and complete as you can. You may find that more than one thing on this list applies to you, but try to focus on one area now, the one that seems most pressing or threatening. What stands in your way, or the character in your story's way, will create tension and conflict for that person or character to solve.

Now that we understand our need for stories, and perceive how we will use them in a concrete way, it's time to look at some of the ingredients for taming our fears. Are you a person who has become comfortable receiving stories from others, either told orally, or through television, films, newspapers, magazines and books? Are you a person who seizes up with fear whenever you recognize that you are afraid of something? Do you need to establish healthier boundaries between your life and the lives of others around you? Maybe you are a person who fears discovering who you really are, for fear that you will not like what you see. Or lastly, maybe you are a person who can welcome fear into your life, and learn that your fear can also become a friend of sorts, protecting you from potential harm while cooperating when you want to try something a bit outside your comfort zone. Choose one of these areas, the one that seems most like you today. You may aspire to one of the others in time, but for this exercise, we're creating a story based on who you are right now. If you'd like, add a line or two to your story, talking about what you would like to change. Taming our fears provides another level of conflict, whether we're working with ourselves or a fictional character based upon our experiences.

Next let's focus on how we can awaken love in our lives, choosing one section from this chapter that most describes where you are now. Are you a righteously indignant person like Elvis Costello, wondering "(What's So Funny 'Bout) Peace, Love and Understanding?" How does that righteous anger galvanize you to action? Are you more focused on achieving peace in your life now? Is most of your life devoted to finding and sending out love? Or are you trying to search for a deeper understanding, of yourself, others, and the world around you? Your stories can be used for any of these purposes, so spend a few minutes thinking about this, and then writing or speaking this part of your story.

Now we'll move from the completely internal to the external in our stories. Have you noticed that you are more of an internal person or an external person? Do you like to think about things before acting, or do you just do whatever you've set your mind to? Are you a person who can take thought and turn it into action? If so, do you notice the Underneath, or the last vestiges or fear, making an appearance sometimes? If so, how does it come about in your life? Is it more of a mental thing, giving you certain thoughts and feelings, or does it manifest physiologically, affecting changes in your body and behavior? Are you a person who has a healthy sense of play? How does this manifest in your life? Do you make time for play, or playfulness, in your daily life? How can it be part of your story? Do you remember what it was like to live outside time? And have you forgot about time recently? If so, what made you forget?

Take a few minutes and choose one of these areas to focus on in your story. Really think about this before you start telling your story. If you need to, spend a few minutes just closing your eyes and breathing to get in touch with the emotions behind each story fragment. Allow little details, such as sights, smells, textures, sounds and tastes to permeate your storytelling, whether it's written or spoken.

Now let's focus on the ghosts that may be lingering at the corners of our lives. These may appear as people we are still afraid to cross, even if they're dead, or voices that stick in your mind, giving you reason you can't do or try something. How did you react to the section on impermanence? Was it freeing for you, or painfully limiting? Are you a person who's drawn to exploring this part of the path a bit deeper, or might you want to look into the universality of stories? Think about your own story for a moment. What makes your story universal and resonant for people who may not have your experience, be of your culture, or live where you live? How can you bridge the gap and communicate with them in a way that seems generous and personal? Are you drawn to the art of listening? Maybe you are a person who prefers to be at the fringes of a gathering, taking everything in and listening to the various conversations, or a person that likes to let other people set the tone. Is this you?

Pick one area where ghosts seem to permeate your life. Whatever you're most drawn to today, choose it and then spend a few minutes getting in touch with why you've chosen that area. Then write in your notebook or speak for a few minutes about your experience. Let your story sing with your own personal stamp.

Lastly, let's focus on the act of waking up to our stories. Are you a person who can let go of disappointment pretty easily, or do you sometimes get bogged down in what you can't do or try? If you can let go, what strategies do you use to let yourself off the hook of these sometimes powerful forces? If you can't let go so easily, what do your inner voices sound like? What have they talked you out of lately? Do you ever feel like you're missing out on part of your life, or are you happy the way you are?

Are you able to cultivate forgiveness, both for others who might have hurt you and yourself, for becoming involved with someone that hurt you? If so, how do you cultivate forgiveness in your life? Are there some things you can forgive, while not being able to forgive others? Are you a person who's attracted to rewriting the script of your life? If you could change anything about your life now, what would it be? Once you have decided that, what steps would you take to help it along the path to fruition?

Spend a few minutes thinking about it, closing your eyes

and breathing deeply for a few minutes if you need to get in touch with the feelings. Pick one of these, and then take a few minutes to write or speak this part of your story.

Now that you have all the pieces of your story assembled, take as long as you need to connect the pieces into a cohesive whole. It does not have to be a perfect, finalized draft right now. If there are rough spots, that's fine. If there are giant holes in the "plot," that's fine, too. The point of the exercise is to get you to see that your stories can be broken down into smaller pieces and then assembled later, using these techniques. I have found, from asking students, that the concept of writing a story from scratch can seem daunting. Hopefully, this lessens the anxiety, and shows you how to "build" a story from the ground up.

When you have finished your story, spend a few minutes just drinking in the feelings of having created what may be, for some of you, your very first story. I like to close my eyes and thank whatever force sent me this story, whether it's my own mind, the Universe, God, the Goddess, or whomever. Just sit in appreciation for a few minutes.

Then take a few minutes to read over or listen to your story again. If you wrote your story, read it over once silently and then read it out loud, giving credence and validation to every single word you wrote. If you spoke your story into a tape recorder, take a moment to play your story out loud from beginning to end, listening carefully and validating every single word you spoke. Rest for a few minutes in the details of your story, knowing that it is your truth, and it has value.

If you'd like to have an additional challenge, try sharing your story with one other person. This is certainly not required, because many people find telling their first story both exciting and sometimes draining. So the thought of telling it to another person may seem overwhelming now. If so, don't worry about it.

For those who may want to give this a try, spend a few moments thinking about who you want to share your story with. Just as we set an intention when starting to write, it's important to consider our intention when deciding to share our stories, and with whom. Are you looking for attention? Validation? Love? Do you want to be taken seriously?

Choose the person you decide to share with carefully. We may have a certain person in mind that we'd like to impress, or get a jolt of admiration from, but this person may be the last one who'd actually give that out. Sharing your stories, especially if you're just starting to do this, can be a very vulnerable thing. Just as you would be vigilant about your feelings when embarking on a relationship with someone you didn't know very well, treat your brand-new story as a fragile parcel.

When you share your story with this person, watch how it makes your feelings change, as well as the sensations in your body. Is this act scary to you? Empowering? Nauseating? A rush?

If you'd like, record how you reacted, as well as the reaction of the person you shared your story with. Was this person supportive of your efforts to tell and share stories? How did he or she demonstrate this? Becoming more aware of the subtle hints people give off in their behavior will only make you a more sensitive storyteller in the long run.

In the next chapter, we will talk about ways to take your storytelling further, making suggestions for exercises you may want to use to keep your mental muscles in shape, and meditations that may help you to develop your powers of observation. You have achieved a great deal so far, and it's completely up to you where you take this practice from here. Whether you want to become a professional storyteller, writing books and articles, making films, or singing songs, or you want to share your personal stories with another generation, you are well on your way to making your life happen, just the way you've told it.

Taking it Further

"To finish is a sadness to a writer - a little death. He puts the last word down and it is done. But it isn't really done. The story goes on and leaves the writer behind, for no story is ever done."

— John Steinbeck

We've come to the end of our journey in waking up to our stories. This week, the focus will be on deciding which direction to take your storytelling endeavors in the future. I will provide a few suggestions to get you started, and leave you with one final meditation exercise to close our practice together.

But first, let's do our weekly check in from last week:

- Were you able to review all of the notes in your notebook, or recordings on your tape recorder, to bring a sense of closure to your practice?

- Did you look over the list of chapter heads and sub-heads, then choose one from each part of the list to make your own mini outline for a personal story?

- Could you see how this outline started to give the structure of a story, with a built-in conflict of fear?

- Did you set your intention before beginning to tell your story?

- Were you able to write down your story, using this mini outline, or speak it into your tape recorder?

- Did you get in touch with your own silence, and the reasons behind it?

- Were you able to understand the need for stories in your life?

- Could you get in touch with how you are likely to use stories in your life, even if it's only in the next part of your life?

- What stood in the way of your telling your personal stories?

- Did you contact your fear, or begin to understand how fear can convince us not to try new things or express ourselves fully?

- How did you go about awakening love in your life? Was there more than one type of love involved, or more than one step required to do this?

- Did you find that you are more of an internal person, or an external person?

- Were you able to awaken your sense of play?

- Did you find yourself existing as if time didn't exist while writing or telling your story?

- What ghosts, if any, did you notice hanging around the edges of your life or your stories?

- Were you able to practice the art of listening? If so, how did that feel for you?

- As you began to tell your personal story, did it feel like part of you was waking up, or coming alive again?

- Were you able to cultivate forgiveness in your story, or in your daily life?

- Were you able to get in touch with the emotional and physical feelings behind each aspect of your story?

- Could you accept that your first draft of this story didn't have to be perfect, just as authentic as possible in your own personal voice?

- What emotions did you experience, especially if this was the first story you've ever written?

- Did you spend some time reflecting on your story, then expressing gratitude at being able to tell it?

- Did you take the additional challenge, and share your story with one other person? If so, did you choose this person carefully?

- Lastly, did you make a mental note of the emotions and sensations that occurred in your body while you shared your story with at least one other person? If so, what were they?

Take a few minutes to record your answer to these questions, knowing that there is no right, there is no wrong. There is only looking inward in order to discover what our stories want to tell us. If they learn to trust that you will treat them with respect, you may be surprised at what they choose to share with you in the future.

Then check in with your mind and your body for a few minutes, noticing if there are any strong emotions or physical feelings in you now. Honor what you find, and dedicate yourself anew to your storytelling practice for this final week.

Healing Your Past

No matter what our backgrounds have been like, each of us has at least one area we'd like to heal. It's the nature of life—things are not always easy or devoid of struggle. Maybe we weren't close to the members of our families, or found it hard to make friends. We may consider ourselves unlucky in love, or doomed in the job market. Each of these represents an area that could be helped with storytelling.

If our lives have been especially traumatic, we may wish to fictionalize them. Giving "our" character another name, or slightly different physical characteristics, gives the character a sense of distance for us. In retelling the stories of our past, these events do not hurt as deeply, or have the power to drag us back into unproductive or depressing thoughts.

Other writers find that memoirs are the perfect form for healing events of the past. Memoirs are somewhat like an autobiography, but they do not have to be chronological, or even reveal the entire scope of a person's life. If you are drawn to telling stories for healing purposes, you may find that concentrating on the summer you lost your virginity is helpful, or even the week you stopped talking to your mother because she forgot to pick you up from school.

Concentrating your efforts around a particular time can be very therapeutic, especially if you have barricaded this part of your life away from where you are now. Employing the meditations and exercises on fear may help to open up this area for you, and adding the material on forgiveness and awakening love will help to structure your sessions into real stories. Once you have gotten in touch with all of the painful scenes from your past, not to mention the feelings and physical sensations you associate with them, you are ready to rewrite these events in the way you wish they had happened. Hopefully, this will set you free, if even just a little bit, so you can continue your meditation and storytelling practices.

Since painful events live as memories in our minds, taming the mind with meditation is likely to have some effect if done over a period of time.

If you are interested in carrying your storytelling practice forward to include healing events from your past, please don't forget that you always have the option of working with a professional therapist, should you feelings become scary or overwhelming.

Nurturing Your Relationships

I have found, from years of talking to groups of students and meditation practitioners, that most of us believe, at least one some level, that once we form a relationship with someone, it takes care of itself. We are not trained to nurture our relationships, especially with friends or family members. Finding love and sexual satisfaction, or job and financial fulfillment, becomes paramount.

But relationships are not robotic things. They are not run by batteries or cords pushed into electrical jacks. They are living things, and like all living things, need nourishment, development, and careful, dedicated nurturing. We may forget to call our friends because we're busy, or fail to make an important family function in the interest of impressing a potential new mate. We have already seen, in our ten weeks of working together, that we are connected in more ways that we know. Our tonglen practice of giving and receiving taught us that much.

Continuing your practice of storytelling can help with nurturing your relationships in a few ways. First, making the time for yourself each day, for your meditation practice and your follow-up exercises, has undoubtedly begun to teach you that you are worth spending time on. Once you have bought into that, you are far more likely to extend the same consideration to your friends and family members. Making

202

time for them is never wrong, especially if you are reinforcing a sense of connectedness and devotion. Loving humanity begins with this simple step.

Secondly, you may choose to share your stories with a friend. Doing so shows this person that you trust him or her, and want to allow this person into a more personally held part of you. If you and a friend can take part in a storytelling practice together, writing stories and then reading them to each other allows you to draw closer together, and also gives you plenty of opportunity to practice the all-important art of listening!

Lastly, we are able to nurture the relationships in our lives, even if the person we wish to nurture is no longer alive, or doesn't exist in our lives yet, by using the meditations and follow-up exercises related to awakening to love. If you want to attract a new love into your life, wake up to the way you think about love, and the way you currently show it to others, then rewrite the story of your life, featuring you as the main character. What does your love look like, and how does he or she act? What does this person do for a living, and what do you do when you are together? Lavishing as much detail as possible on your story gets you that much closer to being able to visualize the person you want to attract. And once you have visualized that person clearly, with the help of your storytelling practice, manifesting this person can't be far behind!

If you want to nurture your relationship with someone who's no longer with us, you may wish to do the meditations and exercises related to ghosts first, to get in touch with how this person may still be affecting your life, in positive and negative ways. If you find ways in which your life is no longer served by holding on to these "voices," you may wish to employ the meditations and exercises on cultivating forgiveness, then choose to rewrite the script of your time together, "correcting" any areas that remain especially painful for you.

Another exercise I find helpful with friends, mates, or relatives that have passed on is to write conversations, where you assume your voice for your part of the conversation, and the departed person's voice for the other. It may be hard to get in touch with this person's "voice," especially if he or she has been dead for some time. But over time, students have found that their unconscious minds take over, and the conversations start to feel a little more like their real conversations with that person.

Asking for What You're Worth

This is a big one for most people. Since most of us are trained not to draw attention to ourselves, but to succeed all the same, we're given mixed messages from the very beginning of our lives. Our urge to tell and share stories may find that same sense of push-pull behind them as a result.

If you've ever worked at any type of job, and most of us have, we know that it's not easy to ask for a raise, or even for the respect you may feel you deserve. Part of you may say, "Take the job, you need the money," or ""Who do you think you are, asking for all that?" or even "If you don't take this job, someone else will, and then they'll be ahead of you." The same thinking can be applied to love, and asking for the type of relationship we really want. These are the times when all of our unconscious buttons are right out in the open, just waiting to be pushed.

Asking for what you're worth is a very rich area for both meditation and storytelling practice. Where money or love are concerned, we immediately have worries about failure, accomplishments, and even survival. If you are drawn towards telling and sharing your stories in order to ask for what you're worth, I suggest that you start with the meditations and exercises on silence. Ask yourself: In what ways am I complicit with my situation, when I do not open my mouth and speak up for what I really want, or feel I deserve? How do I feel about my own visibility? Am I happier being in the background, because it's less pressure, or do I really want to share all I have to share with a partner, a company, a business, or the world?

Next, move onto the meditations and exercises related to what stands in the way of you telling your own personal truths. Do you believe that other people, your potential mate or boss perhaps, tell stories better than you do, and that you deserve to be in the background? Or do you feel that you are worth more, in the way of attention, love, and even money?

When you have gotten in touch with these important foundational feelings, look at the meditations and exercises on taming fears. Do you have a fear of asking for things in general, or just in one area? If it's in one area of you life, what is that area? Love? Money? Attention? How does your silence play into this, as well as your feelings about your own visibility? Rather than getting depressed at what you find, or being additionally hard on yourself, do the meditations and exercises on developing your sense of play. Looking at your silence is not supposed to be an exercise in self-flagellation. You can choose to hurt yourself all over again, or you can choose to move forward. Here's hoping you choose the latter.

Once you have awakened your sense of play, or at least remembered the joy that's present for all of us, somewhere underneath the responsibilities and worries, keep cultivating that. When we reinforce a belief, a behavior, or a style of thinking, we develop karma. This is a word that has been associated with "as you sow, so shall you reap," promising a punishment for evil deeds done. But in reality, karma is the beliefs we form by reinforcing them in our minds: "I'll never get the kind of salary I really want," or "All the great guys are either taken or gay," or "Every time I try to get any kind of attention, my boss always talks over me, or tries to take credit for my work." What we believe really can become our reality, not because of any magical formula, but because it's all we allow ourselves to see.

Finally, if you want to develop strength in asking for what you're worth, look at the meditations and exercises related to letting go of disappointment. Being able to release old beliefs about ourselves, or even the people we come in contact with, frees us to live with a clean slate. When we go into that meeting with our boss, armed with our accomplishments and ability to overcome challenges, we're looking at a person we have no real history with. We can speak directly and without hostility, confident in our ability to state our case for a raise or promotion, sure of our place in the world.

Collecting Family Stories

Collecting family stories is a wonderful way to use your newfound practice of storytelling. It is my fondest hope that writing this book will help to draw people closer together, and to deepen the understanding and humanity between them. If you have a close-knit family, you may find some of the techniques and exercises in this book wonderful for drawing the stories out of other people, who may have the same issues of silence and complicity at the heart of their own upbringing.

Family gatherings, picnics, birthday parties, graduations, weddings—these are all wonderful opportunities to practice your art of storytelling, by sharing the stories you've discovered inside yourself with others. And it's also a wonderful time to express interest in others, by practicing the art of listening and strengthening that part of what you do. Writers are usually wonderful listeners, straining towards the slightest hint of a story. If someone seems bashful, you might try joking around with the person, to loosen them up, or simply stay quiet and allow this person to fill the empty space with his or her words.

If someone doesn't want to share their stories, though, it's up to all of us to be respectful of their privacy. They may be embarrassed, or just unaccustomed to this new practice. That's fine. Let them have their own way of dealing with the stories inside them. It's not for us to proselytize.

Telling family stories can be a wonderful way to leave a living legacy to be passed down from generation to generation. One family I know keeps adding to the tapes they have, so young children are able to hear grandparents they may never have met, and even themselves, when they were much younger. Other families have written the stories down, starting with the oldest ones, and culminating with the ones of the youngest. This is a great way to heal old rifts between people, as they recognize the shared humanity we all share in the words of a story. Some, such as David Sedaris, have found they can make a good deal of money from sharing their family stories, especially if they are humorous in nature. Books, movies or even television shows thrive on these types of stories, because everyone shares an original family, which makes the demographic that much larger.

Self-Publishing

If you decide to collect your stories, or the stories of your friends and family, you might consider trying to get them published, if this is a path that seems rewarding to you. The publishing industry is a hard one to navigate, so most people decide to approach an agent at first, to see if that person will be the broker between the author and the publishing houses.

But if you don't want to go that far, you can always self-publish your stories, by typing them up and using desktop publishing software to lay them out, print them, and bind them together in some way, perhaps with a stapler or three-hole binding of some sort. Some people choose to give these out as family gifts at the holidays, or put them into the world in another way, such as at church gatherings.

Still others may wish to have their stories appear in traditional book form. With some research on the Internet, you may be able to find several printing companies that will print under 100 books, perfect-bound (this is what a traditional paperback has). Holding a published book with your name on it is a wonderful feeling, but it's certainly not the only way to share your stories with other people, so if you're not drawn to this path, it's no big deal.

Joining a Storytelling Group

Sometimes, storytelling is best when shared. One way to deepen your practice is to join with a likeminded person, or group of people, to nurture the art of storytelling. As with going to the gym, motivation is bolstered by having at least one partner. The other person, by just doing the activity alongside you, keeps you going when you're not feeling up to the task. Similarly, agreeing to meet at a certain time and place each week, month or year can keep you going because you know that you are accountable to the other person. A little bit of this shame is okay, as long as it doesn't spill over into more negative emotions, like blame or self-destructive behavior.

When starting a storytelling group, you might wish to begin with your immediate group of friends. There is already a sense of connection between you, which is important, and a degree of interest in what the other person might have to say. Whenever I have done these practices with friends of mine, I have been startled to discover how much I learned about people I thought I knew pretty well.

Remember that sharing a story with anther person may require a great deal of bravery on the other person's part. It may be easy for you, but terrifying for them. Cultivate your art of listening carefully. Don't assume that listening only means turning your ears on and relaxing back into your seat. Try to sense if your partner needs encouragement, if she is slow and stammering, or he needs a little space to find

208

his voice. With concerted effort, we can all learn to become better listeners this way.

If you want to extend your storytelling practice to a larger group of people, please feel free to do so. The groups I know about have the most success when their group has a certain shared theme, such as the desire to heal from past abuse or neglect, or the desire to express themselves to their fullest ability. People who may not be reading their own stories will often recognize a bit of themselves in whatever is being read, so everyone tends to have a more rewarding experience.

Bearing witness to one another's stories can be extremely powerful and extremely overwhelming for those who may not be used to overt displays of emotion. These meditations and exercises tend to release deep-seated fears, joys, and memories. There may be resistance to letting them go, and it's not helpful, as a fellow group member, to point that out to someone. The intention of this book is not to promote a small but dedicated police force, marshaling everyone's storytelling. Rather, it's meant to build a supportive community and a safe place to be for people who want to tell stories. If you are drawn towards starting a group of your own, please establish in the group's ground rules that everyone must be attentive and encouraging. No matter how much you might like to, please do not critique each other's stories at this point.

If someone wants to enter a writing workshop and work on stories there, they are agreeing to be critiqued by each person there. But adding too much criticism at the beginning of this process is only likely to dissuade people from speaking up, which runs counter to the goal of the program.

With that being said, please have fun with your stories. Trade them with friends on the Internet, put them in your personal galleries, along with your pictures and anything else you find creative. Find the joy inside you, which delights in connecting with others.

Dealing with Personal Issues or Challenges

If you chose not to move forward with your new practice of storytelling right away, know that you have it in your arsenal of tools. Using the meditation exercises on taming fear can help you deal with personal issues that may arise in your life, or help you deal with challenges that may have seemed insurmountable in the past. You can also choose to combine them with the exercises on awakening love and cultivating forgiveness to give yourself the foundation you may need to bring this practice off the mat and into your daily life.

Writing is a very solitary discipline, which is why so many have been unhappy and unfulfilled in pursuing this path. But if you are called to it, it can be a very gratifying path as well. Dealing with personal issues and life challenges can be the same way. Your new storytelling practice provides a way to safely explore each, without having to give in to misery or depression.

Adopting a New Art Form

Your storytelling practice does not have to confine itself to the written word. As we have discovered, stories are as much to be spoken as they are to be written, and so it follows that your stories can take many forms. If you have had a secret or not-so-secret desire to dabble or develop your talents in another art form, you may have the confidence to try that now. Taking it further can mean turning your personal narrative into songs, dances, theater pieces, or even spoken word performances.

Some of the best personal stories have been skillfully woven into plays (Arthur Miller's *Death of a Salesman*) and other art forms. If you're not looking for such a large stage, you might try reading your personal stories out loud at family gatherings or funerals, to memorialize someone's life.

210

You have developed yourself, and have new ways to plumb your mind for rich, raw material. What you do with it now is for you to decide. But please, by all means express yourself, in whatever art form you feel most comfortable with.

Building a New History

At the beginning of this book, I made the case for storytelling being not just something that happened to us, but something we are responsible for engaging with as humans. As you continue your storytelling practice, in whatever way you choose, you are adding to the fabric of human history, and rewriting it in a more truthful fashion. You assume a position of power in the cultural dialogue, and contribute your valuable, lasting piece of the puzzle.

Our stories can help us ease racial tensions, religious rifts, or other global misunderstandings. By focusing on the ways we are connected, we reinforce mindful consideration of others. Whether we agree or disagree with their methodologies, we become content to let others live the way we want to live, with dignity and peace, without judgement.

If you choose to, you can take your new storytelling practice to a political place, helping to effect healing on a global level. War and national strife, hunger, animal rights and environmental issues are some of the ways my students have found to engage their personal stories with their wishes for a healthier world.

The point is to keep doing it, while keeping your balance between loose and tight, being honest and finding your edge. Discipline will help you to get it done, but a devoted sense of play will help to open us up to the stories that will keep informing us, if we let them.

Final Meditation:

I'd like to leave you with one final meditation exercise,

to close the practice we've shared for these eleven weeks, and to send you into the future with one more way to wonder at our bewildering, beautiful lives. Thank you for taking this journey with me. I hope to see you in the future sometime, and to hear the stories that spring from inside you. Namaste.

- Find your way to your meditation spot, and make sure you will not be disturbed for at least thirty minutes. Close the door and make sure you have your notebook and a writing instrument, or your tape recorder.

- Let your body find its way into your preferred meditation posture. Whether you are seated cross-legged on a cushion, or in a chair with your feet flat on the floor, take a breath and feel your connection with the earth beneath you. Feel its support, and know that it is always there for you. Let your body find its natural balance, with your body upright and dignified in the posture.

- Now begin to notice your breath as it moves in and out of your body. Rather than controlling your breath, or trying to make yourself a certain way, accept your breath for what it is right now. Let your breath come and go as it will. Allow yourself to be breathed as your body keeps you alive and thriving.

- Observe the way your body is feeling now. Let your attention shift to any areas where you might be holding any tension, or feeling any pain. This is the state of your body right now, and it is fine. Some parts of your body may be able to relax a little more than others, but don't force any part of your body to do what you think it should. Just be.

- When you notice a thought resting in your mind, or even moving through on its way to someplace else, take a moment to label it, saying "thinking," to yourself. Touch your thoughts lightly with your attention as you begin

212

your Base Practice. Let your thoughts arise as they will, then allow them to leave you on your out breath. Take five full breaths here.

- When you are ready, begin to connect each of your senses to your meditation practice. It's amazing that our senses need waking up on a daily or even hourly basis, but they do. Our lives are not usually arranged to allow such luxuries, so take a moment and just label each of your senses in turn, reveling in the luxury of connecting with these senses that bring us so much important information.

- When you have labeled each sense in turn, return to your base Practice. Take five more full breaths in and out. Label your thoughts as you notice them in your mind.

- Now think about a time in your life when you had the sense that the world was bigger than you. It may be a memory from childhood, at not being able to reach something, or being yelled at by the giants who were your parents. It could have happened last week, or yesterday, when something you wanted did not happen the way you had hoped. Get in touch with that moment, the one that seems strongest with emotions right now. Picture that moment in your mind, and let your body register the emotions associated with it.

- Keep this moment in your mind as you look into your body. What kinds of feelings do you have, and where are they localized? How are they different from how your body was feeling at the beginning of the meditation? Do the two seem to have any relationship to one another?

- Now see yourself growing, very quickly, morphing into the person you are now. You may see this like a series of images flashing by—a slideshow of your life. You may experience it transition by transition, using all of your senses. Feel the years going by and the experiences accumulating as you grow into the person you are right now.

- See yourself facing the same challenge you faced then. But now you're the age you are today. How has the path you've tread prepared you to deal with this moment? What does it feel like, in your body and emotions? Take five full breaths here, letting the feelings become conscious.

- When your feelings are completely at the conscious level, label them silently, to yourself. Picture a long road, stretching off into the distance. Don't overthink it, just hold the image of the first road that comes to mind. What does your road look like? Is it a rusty dirt road curving into the desert, or a paved superhighway, teeming with cars?

- Now see yourself on this road, on foot, or in the conveyance of your choice. Where are you going, and what brought you here? Let your feelings work their way through your consciousness and keep breathing.

- Is there something you have put off in order to be here now? Let your innermost thoughts come to the surface, to communicate whatever they want to say. Breathe and let yourself just see you, exactly where you are.

- Did someone convince you to put this off, or did you just decide to do it yourself? Do you still have a desire to do this? Why or why not? Just sit with the feeling that there was some part of you that may have been left incomplete, and may need to be encouraged in order for you to continue growing.

- If you are on foot, imagine that a beautiful car comes to pick you up. It's completely safe, because the driver is someone you know and trust. You get in the car and begin your journey. If you are already driving, picture

214

yourself gaining speed. It's perfectly safe, because the car is handling well, and no one else is on the road.

- Picture yourself arriving at your destination. What does it look like? Who is there? What year is it? In the future, now, or in the past?

- See yourself as you get out of the car. What do you look like? What are you wearing? What kind of event is happening? Try to get in touch with as many details as you can, including sights, smells, sounds, tastes and sensory experiences.

- Now spend ten breaths letting this scene play out in your mind. What do you do once you get out of the car? Who do you gravitate towards and who do you shun? Listen to the words that come out of your mouth, as well as those of the people around you. Is this a festive occasion, or something more somber?

- See yourself doing exactly that thing you may have put off in the past. Even if you have to go into a private room for a minute to do this, take the time for yourself and just do it. See how it feels to do this thing you may have always longed to do. Allow your body to get in touch with the sensations associated with doing this particular activity.

- Take five full breaths, just validating the feelings inside you. Feel the satisfaction of having tried this thing or attempted that challenge that had daunted you all these years. Label your feelings and keep breathing.

- Now bring up the same image we began with, of you, as a grown person, facing the same instance in which the world felt larger than you. How does it feel now? What sorts of emotions are running through you? What sorts of bodily sensations are you experiencing?

- Now see your grown-up self dealing with that situation as an adult would. If you were a child in this situation, let your adult self handle it with maturity and ease. If you were an adult when this situation happened, let your highest, divine self handle it, decisively and with great grace.

- Take five full breaths here, allowing your mental movie to play out in your mind. Now, the world isn't bigger than you. You have all the skills and tools you will ever need to deal with challenging situations, or those in which you feel less than. Know that you don't have to feel diminished or disrespected in any area of your life.

- Check in with yourself emotionally, to see what feelings you're having. Then check in with your body. What emotions are strongest in you now, if any? Are there any places in your body where there is residual tension or apprehension? How has seeing yourself grow up changed the way you were at the beginning of this meditation?

- Bring your awareness to your road again, the same road you saw earlier in the meditation. Where does your road lead? Are you on the road now, or about to step onto it? And what happens next? Spend five breaths here, letting yourself see where you are, relative to where you're going.

- Bring your attention back to your Base Practice, labeling your thoughts as you notice them in your mind. As you notice each one, touch it lightly and allow it to dissolve on your out breath.

- Let your mind return to its normal state, while letting go of any worries, physical pains, or troubled feelings left over from this exercise. Come out of the meditation, vowing to share your stories with others.

216

Resources

Mini-cassette recorders, tapes, and batteries are available through most electronics or big box stores nationwide, and can be purchased online at these stores:

Amazon.com

BestBuy.com

CircuitCity.com

RadioShack.com

Frys.com

Target.com

Also, should you wish to network with other storytellers, the National Storytelling Network holds several conferences around the country, usually during the spring and summer months. There is also a yearly festival, usually held in Tennessee, where the organization is based. For more information on these, as well as other valuable services and programs, go to www.storynet.org.

Acknowledgments

Thank you to my mother for the gift of stories, and to my father, whose acumen I have slowly but gratefully inherited.

Thanks to the writers and artists that have filled me with inspiration and hope. They are too numerous to list, but include Ray Bradbury, Elvis Costello, Joseph Bruchac, Arthur Miller, Daniel Goleman, and William Faulkner, among many others.

To my friends fighting the good fight in the trenches of art, soldier on. Your tenacity in telling your stories, no matter how difficult, amazes me.

Much gratitude to teachers John Rechy and Terry Wolverton, as well as to the participants of their workshops. Their input will always inform my work.

Thanks also to teachers Pema Chodron, Sylvia Bercovici, Thich Naht Hahn, Chogyam Trungpa Rinpoche, Jon Kabat-Zinn, and Candace Pert.

My gratitude extends to my editorial clients, who have taught me a great deal about life and words over the years, and to the colleagues who have broadened my knowledge of storytelling.

A huge hug to the students who have gone through this program with me, and shared their stories so selflessly. May you continue to experience its benefits.

And to Noel, a hell of a writer, ever and infinitely patient, it goes without saying that you rule.

About the Author

Alyson Mead's fiction, essays and articles have appeared in over twenty-five publications, including *Salon.com*, *In These Times*, *Bitch*, *BUST*, the *Whole Life Times*, *Punk Planet*, *MSN.com*, *The Sun*, *AOL.com*, *LA Tribe*, *Rockpile*, *ChickClick*, *Tapestry*, *IRT*, *The Stylus*, and the *New York Daily News*, among others.

She has received the Columbine Award for Screenwriting, the Roy W. Dean Filmmaking Grant, and a *Writer's Digest* Award. Her work also appears in the anthology *Stories of Strength*, benefiting the victims of Hurricane Katrina.

For more information on upcoming releases, tape sets and seminars, or to join Alyson Mead's emailing list, go to www.FindYourProsperity.com.

Wake Up to Your Stories